FOLK ARTS AND CRAFTS

FOLK ARTS
AND
CRAFTS

MARGUERITE ICKIS

ASSOCIATION PRESS * NEW YORK

FOLK ARTS AND CRAFTS

———

———

Association Press, 291 Broadway, New York 7, N. Y.

> The illustrations in
> FOLK ARTS AND CRAFTS
> are by Dr. Miklos Foghtuy

Library of Congress catalog card number: 57-11596

◄◄►55

Printed in the United States of America by
American Book–Stratford Press, Inc., New York

ACKNOWLEDGMENTS

FOLK ARTS AND CRAFTS is the result of browsing through dozens of volumes and searching museums for folk projects that might appeal to the American people. We would like to give credit to the authors and publishers for every single Easter egg and piece of furniture selected but, since there are several hundred items, this is an impossibility. Our whole idea is to present to our people folk crafts decorated with authentic designs in order to give them an appreciation and understanding of other nations. We hope, therefore, that if an article appears that is not in the public domain, its publisher will take pleasure in the fact that it has helped a young nation understand the folk people from which it sprang.

Special credit should be given to two men, Helmuth Theodore Bossert and Charles Holme, who have made the study of European Folk Arts their life work. The works of these men are categorized according to countries and all are beautifully illustrated, including many color plates. A complete book of folk toys by Emanuel Herric was printed in Prague, Czechoslovakia in 1950. The Hungarian National Museum of Folk Arts in 1950 published a book on the Magyar folk crafts, beautifully illustrated in color.

Several books on the Norwegian folk arts have been published in English as follows: Native Arts of Norway, Houghlid and Norway Peasant Arts, Band Bovy.

The author is deeply indebted to Dr. Miklos Foghtuy who so beautifully illustrated this book. He is a native Hungarian and his knowledge of the folk arts in central Europe served as a guide for the selection of authentic crafts. Many of the techniques described are from his memory.

Contents

Introduction

THE PURPOSE of this book is to present authentic folk crafts which can be applied to present day demands, and to tell how to do them. Since they embrace most media used in a recreational craft program, the material suggested should enrich the practical work both as to form and color. Folk crafts stand high among the creative arts and, as means of enjoyment and self expression, you will find them second to none. However, in order to fully appreciate the meaning of the projects and their decorations, it is necessary to look beyond the structure and design to the peasant who made them. What were the thoughts he was trying to express, why did he choose certain colors and is he telling a story? These are the factors that make folk art so fascinating a study.

Folk art is a handicraft of a people who had an innate desire to create and beautify things for their homes and community. Since we are limited as to space, we have selected mostly European crafts because they seemed to fit more naturally into our programs in regard to use and function. The peasant created with limitations both as to tools and materials, so the projects suggested should be found practical from an economic point of view. The limitations of the peasant, in a way, added charm to his work. Each article was functional in line and the colors used in the decorations were of the softest hue because they were extracted from earth pigments and native plants. We hope this book will inspire young craftsmen to follow the natural expression of an untutored people who took whatever material was at hand and made something useful.

1

The peasant created because of necessity, but today people buy the objects they enjoy. It is true that in all gains to society there are bound to be certain losses. A common belief of some people is that the value of a handicraft can be determined by the money it brings, but they have not measured the product by what the creating might have meant to the craftsman. This should be of prime consideration in presenting a craft program to children. Once they have made something useful, from its conception, there will be a satisfaction growing out of it that will exceed any economic return. There should be a balance of benefits between the new and the old—the handicrafts based upon the needs of the people with limited media on the one hand, and the abundance of materials and fine tools to create something beautiful on the other.

Poor Richard said in his Almanac, "Things were done at a time for a purpose. The purpose is forgotten and the things continue to be done." This is particularly true of our handicrafts. We have forgotten the underlying principles which formed the foundation upon which folk arts were built and too many craft programs are based upon the number of articles that can be made in the shortest given time. In this changing world, when we are striving to understand people of other lands, surely a knowledge of their crafts is a happy beginning.

1. *Design and Color*

FOLK ART is the result of tradition and is full of symbolism that has been carried on generation after generation by people in various countries. There have been periods when so great a perfection has been reached in this type of decoration that nothing since has equaled it. Modern craftsmen unsuccessfully strive to attain this perfection since these ancient designs are based on tradition, religion, and the customs of a people. No fine line of demarcation can be drawn to indicate where the peasant art of one country ends and another begins. In general it is of the soil, using common objects such as human figures, flowers, birds and trees as motifs. However, the intellectuals, such as the Greeks and Romans, used geometric designs as did the Egyptians and Persians. The peasant never endeavors to reproduce motifs in their naturalistic forms but rather emphasizes other qualities such a gaiety in color and fanciful qualities.

A peasant's guiding influence was his knowledge of nature which helped him to see the beauty around him. He knew his woods and watched a tree grow to maturity to furnish lumber for his furniture. His sheep gave their coats for yarn and he found clay in his soil for pots. The substance for coloring was taken from the fruits and vegetables in his garden. All this we must understand in order to interpret the meaning of folk art. When we consider his limitations as to materials and space, it was truly a great achievement.

Some of the symbolism in European folk art has been replaced by outside influences and has brought lasting changes. About 1725, examples of Chinese art came to France on Chinese lacquers and wall papers. This style, with its light and playful form, spread to other countries, replacing the symmetry and symbolism of earlier periods. The weavers incorporated geometric figures as a form of folk design heretofore used only in the Near East and Asiatic countries. They developed features such as the star, equilateral triangle and octagon because it was impossible to turn a round corner on the loom. As new media are found and techniques developed, the folk arts will remain with their haunting symbols and story of the development of man.

Figure 1. Persian Rug.

Folk Colors

The colors in a folk craft are most important when it comes to associating them with a certain region or period. An antiquarian can distinguish a piece of furniture by the background colors rather than the motifs in the design. This is because earth pigments are peculiar to countries in which they are found and the peasant did not travel far afoot. Dyes were also extracted from native plants and countries bordering on the sea found color in shells and seaweed. Another key to the colors used in various regions is to study the royal coats of arms and note the various color combinations. A peasant was not allowed to incorporate these in his designs and hence we seldom find black, gold or purple in a folk decoration.

However, it is the softness of tone and blending of colors that gives beauty and charm to a folk design. The dry earth colors were mixed with various media, a favorite being skimmed milk. The casine in the milk formed a very hard coating that has preserved the colors and designs for several centuries. The peasants had a custom of making holes in beds of brooks during dry seasons into which, when the rains fell, all sorts of mineral and vegetable substances were deposited and left to act upon each other. The results made colors in great varieties of beautiful shades that cannot be duplicated in a modern laboratory.

Figure 1. Persian Rug. The design of a Persian or Turkish rug is made up almost entirely of symbols tied together with geometric lines as shown in the illustration. The small motifs depict birds, flowers, rain, sunshine, animals, tents, or any story the weaver wishes to tell. The final effect is pleasing because there is perfect balance in the design brought about by equal distribution of colors and weight in motifs. We suggest you look at a Persian rug carefully and study each motif in the design and enjoy the beautiful soft colors extracted from native plants. It is, perhaps, the purest example of what we call folk art. The rug illustrated in Figure 1 is a typical example.

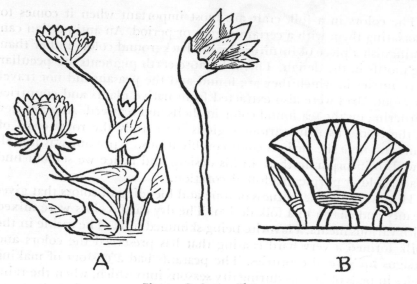

Figure 2. Lotus Flower.

We have developed this introductory chapter to explain some of the symbols once used to express things and now copied only as design or decoration. Surprisingly, the oldest designs known to man were stylized and correspond to those favored by modern artists today. Note the two Egyptian versions of the beloved lotus flower. Figure 2A shows a realistic flower with leaves floating on top of water, while B is a conventional flower design conceived in 1350 B.C. The lotus growing out of water has a second meaning, a thing of beauty growing up out of its murky, impure setting. So, it is necessary to interpret a story as well as symbols in order to fully understand a folk design.

In a peasant design, one rarely finds two motifs cutting across each other. They are usually spaced apart or just touching. In European countries, the subjects of the motifs are much the same, the most popular being birds, trees, flowers, hearts, and often a horse or stag is added for interest. Folk ornament can be divided into three groups and, by giving examples of each, we hope to give you some understanding in our limited space. They are as follows:

Geometric: *Straight lines.*

Naturalistic: *Leaves, flowers, birds, etc.*

Conventional: *Arrangement of motifs to fit need and fancy of designer.*

Figure 3. Greek Designs.

Greek and Roman designs used geometric forms for decoration, an intellectual approach to the earlier Egyptian designs using straight lines and figures in absolute profile. The Greeks were able to soften these figures, show a front view of a face, and give better perspective to hands and feet. Earth pigments, brown, black, yellow, red and grey, were used for colors.

Figure 4. Naturalistic Designs.

Since the peasant based his designs on a knowledge of nature and the out of doors, most European art comes under the naturalistic category. While it is true that the craftsman used natural motifs in his design, it required a great deal of skill to arrange a composition that would fit a given area and have balance as to weight and color (*See Figure 5*). This was done by placing the main motifs in their proper place and then connecting them with curved lines and green leaves.

Figure 5. Floral Design for Chest.

Figure 6. Bird Forms.

Conventional designs were used to form the decoration for a given area. Such devices as placing large flower forms in little pots were used and stylized objects such as the butterflies in Figure 7. This type of design was used by master craftsmen.

Figure 7. Conventional Butterfly Borders.

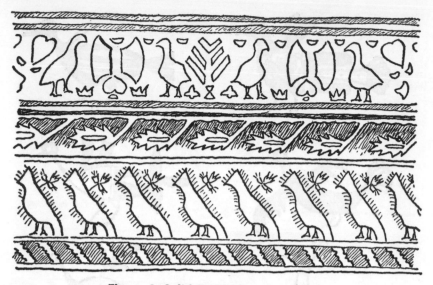

Figure 8. Solid Design from Borders.

A number of borders placed together make an interesting "all over" design for embroidery or textiles. This device is particularly suitable for stencil work as the design can be applied in small sections. They are also very effective on leather belts or purses.

Figure 9. Austrian Border Designs.

Figure 10. Textile Designs.
A—Greek, B—Egyptian, C—African, D—Peruvian, E—Turkish, F—Rumanian.

Figure 11. Borders for Framing.

One of the charms of a folk decoration is that it is not always symmetrical, yet has perfect balance as to weight and interest. Figure 11 shows some examples of interesting framing of a picture where each of the four sides are either different in size or carry separate motifs.

Flower Arrangements

Flowers were, perhaps, the favorite motif for European folk design. Among the flowers most commonly used were the rose, tulip, passion flower, pomegranate, cornflower and carnation. Many of the flowers had religious significance. The rose of Sharon and rosa mundi are used even today as religious symbols. The tri-petal tulip, used so often in German, Bavarian and later in Pennsylvania Dutch designs represents the Trinity. The passion flower symbolizes the crucifixion. The pomegranate goes back to the decoration of Solomon's temple, and the robes of the high priest.

These flowers were not only used as symbols, but the number of flowers in a group also had symbolic significance, three for the Holy Trinity, seven for the creation of the earth, nine (the square of three) for the Trinity. Throughout the world, odd numbers have been considered lucky.

Frequently we see them combined with the whirling wheel or swastika; a sun symbol; or the dove, symbol of the Holy Spirit; or the lamb, symbol of Christ.

In other words, folk art and design often represented a spiritual outlet in lives that were usually hard, drab, and full of drudgery.

13

Figure 12. Cut Paper Designs.

Very little is written on the art of paper cutting. It was first used in the Orient by the embroiderer who covered the delicate designs with silk floss. Later on, cut paper designs were used either for pasting on silk to embroider over, or on walls as charms.

The designs are cut free hand with scissors. The advantage of cutting the design rather than drawing it is that several can be cut at a time and the paper can be folded in half or quarter and all the folds cut at the same time.

**Fig. 13.
European Folk Figures.**

Here is an interesting contrast in figures as they are expressed in Europe and Mexico. Those in Figure 13 have details in their faces and clothing and a great deal of action is expressed by their postures. The Mexican figures are more primitive and few details show in the body and face.

Tree of Life Design.

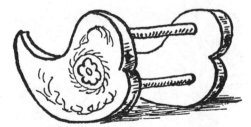

Heart Decorations.

17

Peasant Designs for Woodwork.

These designs are particularly suitable for wood and you may use many and
varied colors.

2. Folk Crafts for the Home

WOOD IS THE FAVORITE material of the peasant worker. Out of it he can fashion simple furniture and express himself by decorating it in accordance with its function and in his native style. People today have something to learn from the simplicity and restraint of the peasant art. One lesson it teaches is that decoration, when used appropriately, blends so well in our modern homes. It is wrought by hand and has nothing in common with mass production which can offer no substitute for the intricate designs and colors.

The decorative processes are of many kinds and vary in different countries. The three most widely used devices are painting on wood,

Figure 1.   **Figure 2.**
German Chair and Foot Stool.

This style of chair can be made in any height from a high stool to a slipper chair. Since the outline has interesting curves, small motifs are used in the design.

chip carving, and wood carving, all of which we will describe in this chapter. Each process can be most primitive in nature, or developed to a very high degree by skilled craftsmen. The most primitive and ancient decoration was to simply score or scarify the wood with a graving tool. Next was what we call "notch or chip carving," used to decorate kitchen utensils, washing sticks, spinning wheels, picture frames, etc. Other decorations were executed in high or low relief in geometric patterns. On a higher plane, we find fluted work and beautiful inlays of ivory and semi-precious stones. The Italians used wood inlays, or in many places rosin and sealing wax were used as a substitute. An offshoot of this was the filling up of intaglio ornaments with a dark colored wax, a process used primarily in the Tyrol. Straw inlay was used in Romania and poker painting was used by the herdsmen and gypsies.

Figure 3.
Peasant Cupboard.

By removing the glass doors from an old cupboard you may convert it into a pleasing piece of furniture. Add a frame and scallops cut from plywood to the front of the shelves.

Figure 4. Design for Hiding Door Knobs.

How to Paint on Wood

You may have an old piece of furniture with good basic lines which you wish to redecorate, or you may find such an article suggested in the following pages. In either case, there are certain steps you must take as follows:

1 **Prepare surface for painting.** This means to bare the wood if it is already covered with old paint or varnish. There are several good paint removers on the market for this purpose so just follow the directions on the container. If it is not necessary to remove an old finish, be sure all wax and grease spots are eliminated and fill all the cracks with a wood filler. Smooth the edges and surface with a fine sandpaper until all scratches are removed.

2 **Apply an undercoat.** The grain of the wood must be filled with a coat or two, depending on coarseness of wood, of shellac or thin varnish. Allow it to dry overnight and smooth with fine steel wool. Do a final dusting with a cloth dampened in turpentine.

3 **Paint in background.** You need a well-finished background before the designs are applied. Decide on the color you want (blue is the peasant's favorite color) and paint the surface carefully with enamel, adding a second coat if necessary. Remember, everything will be toned down by antiquing later so don't worry about using vivid colors. Another favorite background, of course, is white because every color can be contrasted in the design and a coat of burnt umber gives it the appearance of old ivory.

Figure 5. Chest of Drawers.

4 Apply Design. You will not lack design suggestions if you look through the pages of this book. However, you may want your article to dictate the design, with lines and mass to fit the space. If you are doing over a chest of drawers, you may want to treat it in one large design, ignoring the drawers, as shown in Figure 5. Your choice of design can have almost any theme. Just tie it together by using the same colors. Figure 5 shows how a floral design can be used to hide knobs of a drawer. Sometimes, however, the knobs can become an important accent in a design and you may want to emphasize them with a different color.

5 Antiquing. This process makes a newly painted article look old or mellow and softens the tones on newly decorated surfaces. To do this mix some burnt umber oil paint in a dish of turpentine and apply to the surface with a soft brush. Remove excess stain with a rag or sponge. You will have to experiment to see how much burnt umber to use, or if you get the mixture too dark, just wash it off with some turpentine before it dries. This is an excellent way to get highlights on parts of the background to give a more interesting effect. You may want to add a little burnt sienna to the stain to give a glowing effect or use a raw umber for a lighter effect.

6 Add Hard Surface. You must protect the design and antiquing by giving the surface a coat of hard varnish. Get a clear, hard varnish and add a few drops of linseed oil to prevent it from drying too quickly. If you want a dull finish, use a flat varnish or rub down the surface with pumice or fine steel wool.

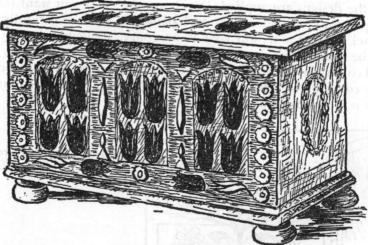

Figure 6. Dower Chest.

In this the embroidered treasures of the dowry were kept by a young bride.

Figure 7. Peasant Chairs.

The backs of these chairs were cut with interesting contours and curves and then the design was made to fit the different areas. Quite often the main motif would be a national flower or family emblem.

Figure 8. Peasant Table and Designs.

This is a pleasing table in its line and balance. Notice the foot rail at the bottom.

Figure 9. Spoon Rack.

Design the plate rack and spoon holder first of all to fit the wall space. Then consider the number of dishes and spoons to be displayed. Cut a pattern from brown paper and use it as a guide in cutting the lumber. Use a good quality of pine, smooth the surface and edges, and decorate each piece before gluing them together.

You may paint the design directly on the wood, thus having a plain natural wood background, or you may cover each piece with a coat of enamel. We think it more interesting to use a variety of designs as shown in illustrations 9 and 10, rather than carrying the same motif throughout. If you do this, you should cut a stencil of the main motifs in order to apply the designs. If you create the designs as you go along, be sure to use the same colors and approximately the same size motifs in order to unify the pieces.

Figure 10. Plate and Cup Rack.

Figure 11. Dough Box.

Figure 11. Dough Box. This colorful tub or box can be used for many other reasons than the making of bread. A large barrel can be sawed in two, leaving a handle on each side and decorated for a wood box.

Figure 12. Salt Box. This style box is easy to construct since the walls form a square.

Figure 13. Mirror. A very handsome mirror can be made by adding a wooden frame and painting with peasant designs.

Figure 12. Painted Salt Box.

Figure 13. Painted Mirror.

Chip Carving

Chip carving is a decorative device that has been practiced by people in all parts of the world. In most museums will be found examples of Dutch, Scandinavian, Egyptian and Chinese work showing the scope of this craft. Probably, because a simple cutting knife is the only tool needed to create the most intricate designs, it is one of the most primitive of the folk arts.

Most chip carving designs are based upon geometric patterns and, by arranging the patterns of these chips, we arrive at a complete design. The area to be decorated is first blocked off and then divided into small units into which the triangles are placed ready for chipping or carving. The final unit might be a square, circle, rectangle or border, according to the plan of the designer.

If you wish to try your hand at chip carving, bass wood is by all means the best material to use. It is a soft, fine-grain wood, so that the chips fly out without splintering when the cut is made. Pine or poplar can also be used, as well as some of the hard woods such as apple or mahogany. Whatever wood you choose, be sure it is perfectly dry and well seasoned.

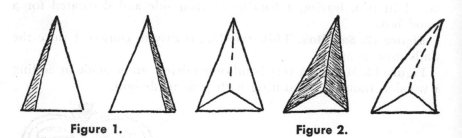

Figure 1.   Figure 2.

In order to lay out a pattern for cutting, you must first understand how to indicate which part of the design is to be chipped away and which is to be left standing in relief. There are two types of cuts, the single triangle and the double triangle. In the single triangle pattern, the part that is to be cut away is darkened. The dotted lines in the double triangle indicate where the cutting is to take place, and the unbroken lines are the ones that will appear raised in the finished work.

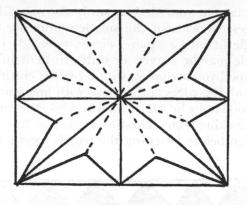

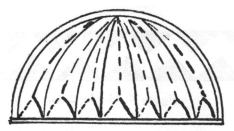

Figure 3. Chip Carving Designs.

Peasants in most European countries decorated kitchen utensils and washing apparatus in solid chip carving designs. The above cuts were taken from a Dutch mangle.

Before you lay out your design, study the ones illustrated on the following pages. Notice that the smallest unit is either a single or double triangle fit into a square, circle, rectangle or triangle. The double triangle may be curved in order to fit it into a given area. Prepare the wood you are going to use by first cutting it into panels and then smooth the edges and surface with fine sandpaper. Remember that the wood must lie flat on a table while the carving takes place so, if you are making a box, chest or a piece of furniture, be sure to carve the design before fastening the panels together.

Figure 4. Single Cuts.

If you are making your first attempt at chip carving, you should make a practice board of bass wood and try all the cuts shown above. Note the shaded parts. These are the parts to be cut away. You will be amazed at the various patterns attained by simply rearranging a number of single triangles.

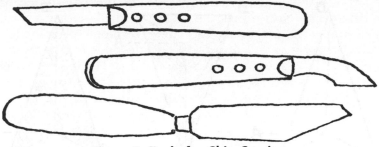

Figure 5. Tools for Chip Carving.

Tools. Chip carving is usually accomplished by using two types of knives as shown in Figure 5: A knife with a short blade cut off diagonally across the bottom and used for outlining the cut. A slicing knife with a curved blade for cutting away the chips and a stencil knife that may be substituted for both the stick and cutting knife if they cannot be obtained.

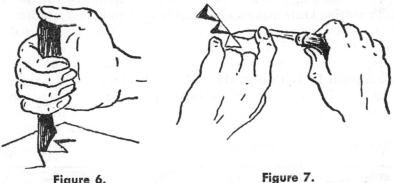

Figure 6.   **Figure 7.**

The Single Cut. Assuming that your design is drawn on your wood, take the stick knife, being sure to hold it in the manner shown in Figure 6. The position of the thumb is important. Place the top of the knife at the apex of the triangle and press it in to whatever depth cut you wish to make. Now pull the blade toward you and complete the cut to base of triangle. Be sure you have a graduated slope, deep at the apex and shallow at the base. Repeat this operation along left side of triangle. Now take the slicing knife, holding it in your hand as shown in Figure 7. The left index finger controls the blade and does all the work. The two middle fingers of the left hand are bent under so they will not cast a shadow. You start always from the original side line of the triangle and go all the way across until you get the desired depth, otherwise your cut will not be clean and smooth. It usually requires two cutting operations to remove one chip.

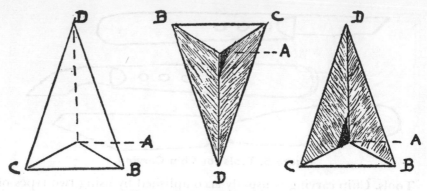

Figure 8. Detail Double Cut.

The Double Cut enables the chip carver to elaborate and refine his work.

Begin the double cut at the point marked A in the left hand triangle in Figure 8. The base of the triangle should be towards you. With a cutting knife make an incision from A to B, and another from A to C. Then turn your work around (center triangle) and make an incision along the dotted line, A to D. The cut should be deep at the top of the small triangle and gradually become shallow as it reaches point D. With your slicing knife, beginning at the right side of the long incision, take out about half of the first long chip and then remove the rest of the wood in as many cuts required to make a clean cut. Now turn your work around again as shown in the right hand triangle and remove the chip in the same manner.

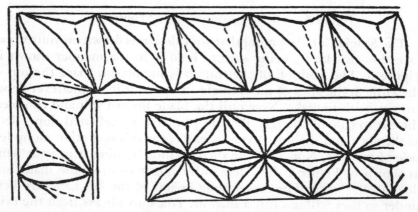

Figure 9. Practice Cuts.

Transfer these patterns to a practice board and remove the chips before attempting a finished project.

30

Figure 10. Chipped Designs from German Chest.

Classic Border Designs.

Some classic traditional patterns—Greek, Roman and Egyptian—detailed for chip carving.

Wood Carving

Wood carving was practiced as a decorative technique in every country in the world and fine examples are always to be found among the folk arts. There are many types of carving for all degrees of skill and talent and the tools employed are few and inexpensive. The craft includes decorating of all types of furniture, paneling of rooms, wooden utensils and the shaping of wooden bowls, toys, and so forth. The designs can be most elaborate or mere chisel marks made in rhythmic repetition, according to use or the ability of the craftsman. Large tools give decisive cuts and are easier to handle by the craftsman.

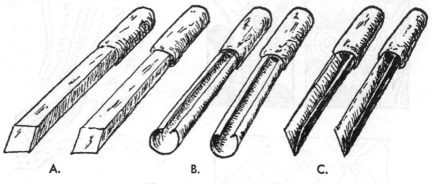

Figure 1. Cutting Tools.

To become a skilled wood carver, one must spend many hours of practice in order to handle the tools deftly and know how to cut against the different grains of the wood. However, there is always a beginning and the purpose of this chapter is to introduce you to the necessary tools and how to use them. Wood carving tools come in many shapes and sizes so you will have to choose a few at first and add to them as the work progresses and the need arises. You may purchase a set of six or eight tools, but the chances are they will not be the size or shape you would like once the work is under way.

In general, you will need the cutting tools illustrated in Figure 1. These consist of

A. Chisels in various widths. They have a flat blade and are used to make a straight cut or line. They are also used for outlining a design and removing background.

B. U gouges. These have curved steel blades and are used when curved stabbing cuts are desired.

C. V gouges. These are very important tools for making connecting lines, deep impressions in a design, and detailed work.

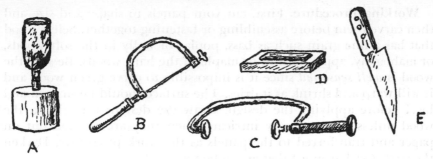

Figure 2. Other Tools.

There are certain other tools you will need in doing wood carving but if you are a craftsman, you may already have them in your tool chest. They are as follows:

A. Wooden Mallet. These come in various shapes, but the one illustrated above is most satisfactory if you are planning to make your own. It should be made of hard wood, preferably maple, and weigh at least a pound. Be sure to design a handle of shape and size to fit your hand.

B. Coping Saw. This is used for outlining an object. It will cut around a curved line, thus saving many hours of hard cutting away with cutting tools.

C. C-Clamps. These clamps come in various widths and are used for clamping panels to a table for carving. This is important as the panel must be held firmly in place while the cutting tools are being struck with the mallet.

D. Oil Stones. An India oil stone with concave, convex and flat surfaces is used for keeping sharp edges on cutting tools. Also, keep an Arkansas stone for general use.

E. A Cutting Knife. A stencil knife or one with a noncollapsible blade can be used to remove much of the wood before shaping tools are required.

A small plane is also useful for smoothing surfaces in preparation for carving.

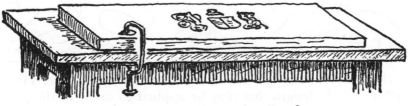

Figure 3. Panel Clamped to Bench.

Working Procedure. First, cut your panels to shape and size and then carve them before assembling or fastening together. Select wood that has a fine grain such as bass, poplar or holly in the soft woods, or mahogany, apple, walnut or maple in the hard woods. Be sure the wood is *well seasoned* since it is impossible to carve green wood and it will warp and shrink as it dries. The surface should be smooth and level before applying the design. Draw the designs directly on the wood unless they are very intricate—then they are worked out on paper and transferred to the panels as the work progresses. Darken the parts (background) that are to be removed.

When the design is drawn, clamp the panel to a table or bench as shown in Figure 3. This is a safety measure, and another measure to be observed is to keep the tools sharp at all times. Always keep hands behind cutting edge of tool while it is in action.

The first step in carving is to outline the design. This is done by holding a chisel straight up and down and striking it with a mallet. When levels are decided upon and rough modeling done, the next step is to smooth the edges. Use a flat U-gouge for this, taking light slicing cuts with the grain.

Avoid undercuts as much as possible in your design. The design becomes weak and will break no matter which way the grain of the wood runs.

The above border designs are excellent for a beginner. They are authentic folk designs that may be applied to many of the projects found on the following pages.

Incised Carving

This method of carving resembles chip carving in that the design is made by incisions in wood to different depths while the surface remains the same. In chip carving the wood is removed in small triangular chips thus forming geometric designs. Incised cuts form grooves, troughs with rounded or v-shaped bottoms, or various shaped depressions. Only a fine-grained soft wood is used for this carving and basswood is by all means the most suitable.

The first step is to cut along the center of all parts to be cut as groove or v-shaped troughs. The more detailed work of rounding and smoothing the design is done with different size gouges. It is easier to make smooth cuts if the larger ones run with the grain of the wood. Try to match the curve of tools to curves in design as much as possible.

The next step is to make slicing cuts. The V-gouge is indispensable in this operation where curves and lines are required. On circular cuts, approach the groove from one angle and then another by turning the work around.

This type of carving is perhaps the easiest technique used in decorating wood. The designs can be delicate and easily executed. Incised carving is used most successfully for butter molds and cookie cutters. See Figs. 5 and 6. A simple design cut into the wood will result in raised designs on butter or pastry dough.

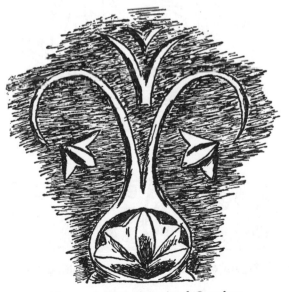

Figure 4. Detail Incised Carving.

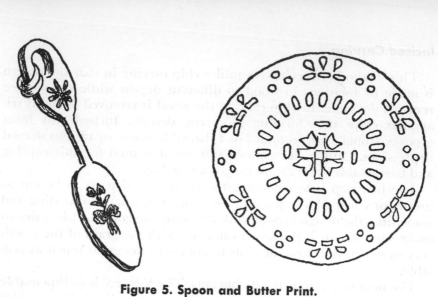

Figure 5. Spoon and Butter Print.

Figure 6. Cookie Cutter and Rolling Pin.

Figure 7. Carved Hungarian Chairs.

The chair in lower right hand corner is from the illustrator's home.

Figure 8. Detail Design.

Carving in High and Low Relief

When a design stands above a sunken background, it is known as relief carving. This method of carving was most commonly used among the folk people as only a few elementary tools were required. Also, the furniture was made up of straight panels which were easily decorated before their assembly into a complete project. Notice that the backs of the peasant chairs have no curves and the dower chests were made in separate panels and glued together after they were carved.

To carve in relief, the following steps must be taken:

1. Cut panel to shape, smooth the wood and draw on the design. Darken the background or area to be cut away. Consider the grain of the wood and plan the long cuts in the design to run lengthwise with the grain.

2. Fasten the panel to a table or bench with C-clamps. Now make vertical stop cuts around the entire motif. This is done by striking a chisel with wooden mallet. Try to keep an even depth around the entire design.

3. Make slanting slicing cuts through the waste wood to remove it. Remove the entire background so that the design stands up in relief. Make the long cuts with your chisel and detailed ones with your gouges.

4. After the background is smooth, the shaping of the standing parts begins. This must be done carefully by using gouges, especially the V-gouge for the lowest grooves.

5. Smooth the entire panel with light cuts and avoid the use of sandpaper as much as possible. A few tool marks, if not too deep, will add to the charm of being hand made.

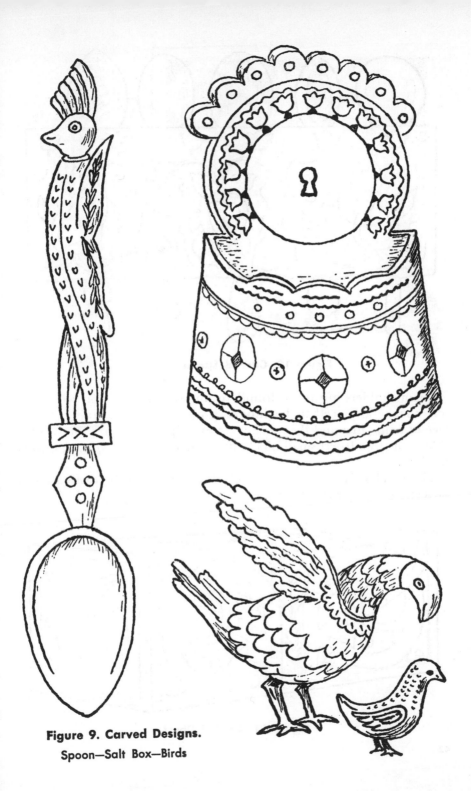

Figure 9. Carved Designs.
Spoon—Salt Box—Birds

Figure 10. Carved Spoon Holder.

Spoon holders are to be found in almost any book on folk arts. They make an excellent beginner's project for woodcarving. Carve face of panel first and then tack a small strip of wood on the reverse side at the top. Insert small blocks of wood at intervals to hold spoons in place.

Figure 11 shows a simplified folk design that can be easily carved on a chest or other wooden panels.

Figure 11. Carved Chest.

A. English Heraldry.

B. French Fleur-de-lis.

C. Ancanthus. Greece.   D. Lotus Flower. Egypt.   E. Lily. Biblical.

Figure 12. Carved Flowers.

Flowers have always played a symbolic part in designs used by both royalty and peasants. The flowers are usually conventionalized when used in wood carving to simplify the technique.

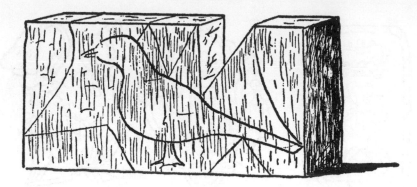

Carving in the Round

To accomplish this type of carving, select a block of wood with the allover measurements of the object you wish to make. Use a fine grained wood such as basswood, holly, maple, walnut, apple, pear or mahogany. These have enough strength in all directions to hold together and will not split open ahead of the blade.

First, trace out a profile of the figure you wish to carve and then, using carbon paper, transfer it onto the wood. Be sure to lay out the design with the grain of the wood running the length of the figure. Now indicate the features on either end of the wood block and on the opposite side. Next take off all surplus wood with a coping saw as indicated in the lines around the above figure. It is easier to cut out wedges that to saw around a curved line.

You are now ready to shape the figure. A good deal of creative imagination is needed for ability to visualize the finished project. When the surplus is taken off, first round off the corners and the outline of the back and head. Carve from the head down. Rough out the body first with large curved gouges and use the flat gouges for surface finishing.

Figure 13. Carved Animals and Birds.

Figure 14. Carved Figures from Tyrol.

These figures can be finished by adding color with oil or wood stains. They can also be left in a natural wood finish by giving them two coats of shellac and waxing them. Another good way to finish is to soak the figure in boiled linseed oil for several days and then dry and polish with powdered pumice or a talcum powder.

Figure 15.
Carved Drinking Cups and
Spoons.

47

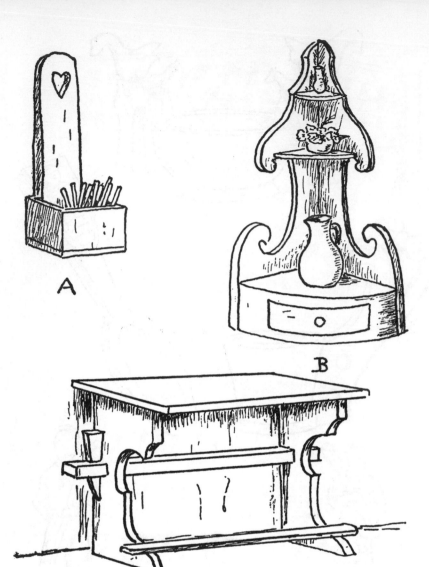

Figure 16. Undecorated Peasant Furniture.

A. **Wall Match Holder.** This had a long holder so it could be hung on the wall above the stove, or be suspended from the mantle to reach the fireplace. Decoration is optional.

B. **Corner Shelf.** An interesting Swedish design that can be made in any size.

C. **Wall Table.** Suitable for a small room or dinette where the table must stand against the wall or in front of the window. Note shelf at bottom for a foot rest.

Figure 17. Greek Furniture.

This book shelf and bench is included in this chapter to contrast the straight lines used in the designs with the more ornate ones used in central Europe.

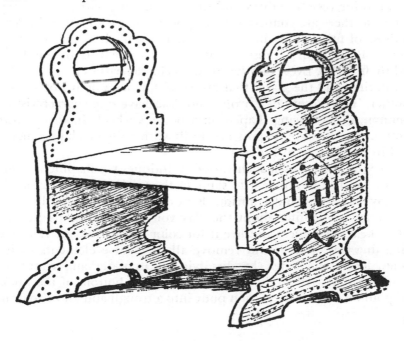

Figure 1. Covered Dish.

POTTERY

Pottery is one of the very oldest of the folk crafts, rising out of the need for vessels to carry and store food. There are as many types of pots as there are countries, from pots of coarsest texture in Africa to those of finest china in France and England. It is easy to classify pottery as to origin because of native clays and nature of the designs and their colors. Every clay has its own characteristics as to shrinking and drying, and the glazes that are good for one might not work on another. The pottery of Europe and Asia have one characteristic in common, that of being shaped on a potter's wheel. In this country, many of the hand-built pots are built with coils of clay, a method used by the American Indians.

Since the potters used such varied techniques for shaping and glazing, we must limit our text to some of the methods used for shaping the clay and adding a decoration. First of all, in exploring these, you must know something about the clay you are going to use; so why not make a test project and fire it for color and shrinkage. If you are using dug clay, you should remove all the coarse elements such as stones, leaves and twigs, by dissolving it in water and running it through a sieve. Allow the clay to settle to the bottom of the bucket and pour off excess water; then pour into a trough and allow to drain.

Figure 2. Thumb Pots.

Methods of Shaping Pottery

Thumb Pots. This is a very primitive method of shaping a bowl or dish. A lump of clay is taken in the hand and rolled into a ball by holding it between the palms. A hole is made in the center with the thumb and the walls squeezed out to form a deep dish. Both the thumb and fingers are used to thin the wall and base to an even thickness and rim.

The Japanese are most adept at this method of shaping a bowl or cup. Their sensitive fingers can thin the clay to a shell-like wall. Figure 3 shows a Japanese cup and dish.

Figure 3. Japanese Thumb Dishes.

Figure 4. Hungarian Water Pitcher.

The Potter's Wheel has been used for centuries in almost every country in the world. The advantage of the wheel is that the clay to be used for the pot remains stationary on the disc and moves around and around while the hands are more or less still. It is also a much speedier process of shaping than the coil method of building layer by layer.

In order to make pots successfully on a wheel, a potter must spend many hours throwing clay for practice in shaping. We do not have space to describe the equipment needed and a plan of a wheel, but it is a most satisfying hobby and we suggest you get a book on the subject.

Such projects as bowls, plates, cups and saucers, teapots and pitchers are usually shaped on a wheel. This is especially true if they are to be made in quantity. The Hungarian water pitcher in Figure 4 was shaped on a wheel and the spout pinched in with the fingers. The handle was cut from a slab of clay, scratched and pressed into the jug and sealed at top and bottom by adding an extra roll of clay.

Figure 5. Slab Pots.

Slab Pottery. This method is used for making vessels which have flat bottoms and where the angles of the walls are the essence of the design. Make a cardboard pattern of your pot according to the pieces required. Roll out the clay on the reverse side of oil cloth with a rolling pin. Make it approximately ⅛" thick for small objects and thicker for larger ones. Be sure to have the same thickness throughout.

Lay your pattern on clay and mark lightly around the edges. Remove the bottom piece first by cutting with a knife and transfer it to a board. Now cut out the other pieces and lay them *around* and not *on* the bottom, ready to be joined. Score the edges of the base and press a soft roll of clay into each corner. Next score edges of walls and press further rolls of clay into them and then assemble the pot. The extra rolls will make the inside corners rounded thus giving strength to the walls. Use ample slip, (clay thinned with water to the consistency of cream) to seal the edges together.

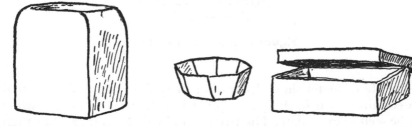

Figure 6. Slab Projects.

Figure 7. Decorated Plates.

The above plates show decoration in typical folk designs. There is a certain charm in designs applied in a free-hand manner which can be seen in each plate. The rhythm and balance is there, but there is no repetition of motif.

Figure 8. Sculptured Figures.

Modeling Clay. A popular use of clay has always been the modeling of small figures. Since no center armature can be used for support, the figure itself must be sturdy enough to stand alone.

Begin with the amount of well-firmed clay you plan to use for the body and shape it into the general proportions. At this point, hollow out the inside as much as possible to aid the drying process later on. Model the features with modeling tools and add extra pieces by rolling small balls of clay and pressing in place carefully with the hand.

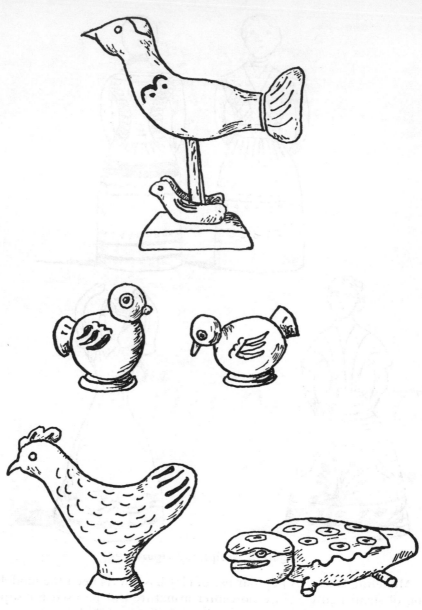

Figure 9. Sculptured Animals and Birds.

Animals should be in a sitting or recumbent position in order to avoid appendages that do not fit close to the body. The mother bird standing above her young is an example of how *not* to make the legs, but we couldn't resist the figure.

56

How to Make Tiles

Tiles offer an opportunity to the potter to apply a decoration in more ways than do any other form of pottery; therefore, they rank high among the folk arts. Underglazed designs are most frequently used, but the decoration can be incised, modeled or inlaid as well.

The greatest drawback to tile making is their tendency to uneven shrinkage resulting in their not lying flat on a table. To avoid this, it is necessary to construct a tile box as follows:

For a single tile 3" x 3", cut two squares of wood just a little larger to allow for shrinkage of clay. Now cut a hole 1" in diameter in the center of one square. Nail a frame or sides ½" high around this square. The other square is to be used as a false bottom when the box is in use.

Place the board in the bottom of the box and dampen all parts of the interior with water; then sprinkle with silver sand to prevent sticking. Now put in a ball of clay, flatten out with the fingers and add more until the box is completely filled. Smooth off the top by passing a ruler over it. The false bottom is then pressed out with the thumb, the tile removed and set aside to dry.

Just before the tiles are dry, stack them in a pile by placing a plaster slab between to absorb any moisture that may be left. Place a heavy weight on top. Another method is to simply turn the tiles from time to time.

Figure 10. Tile Box.

Figure 11. Decorated Tiles.

Here are four tiles showing typical designs applied by the following processes:

A. Colored Slip.

B. Incised Lines.

C. Inlaid Design.

D. Under Glaze.

Figure 12. Money Banks.

Money banks can be found in almost every European country and their design usually has a sense of humor to appeal to children. The slits at the top are of width and length to fit native coins. The cow feeding her calf is a very old bank often used as an illustration of primitive art. Piggy banks are made in Mexico and loved by the children.

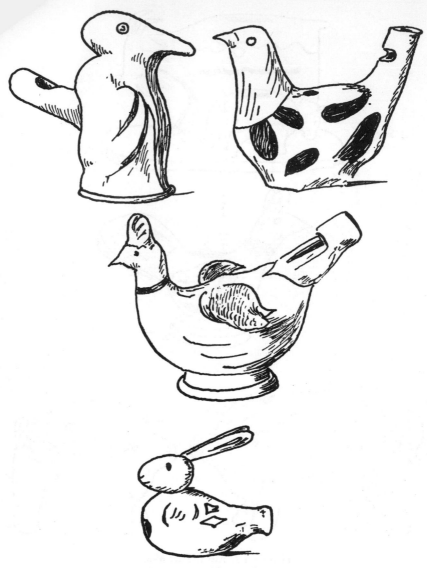

Figure 13. Clay Whistles.

These are clay whistles from Slovakia. The bodies are hollow, but the mouthpieces are made with a small window about 1″ from the end as shown in the illustration. The whistling noise is made by blowing air against a sounding board as described on page 161—How To Make A Whistle.

Figure 14. Austrian Jar.   **Figure 15. Transvalia Mug.**

Methods of Decorating Pottery

Folk pottery is as pleasing in decoration and line as modern articles made today. Decoration was placed appropriately on the object following the natural lines of the pot. The favorite motif was flowers or birds surrounded by a border of simple lines and dots. Many mugs and plates were decorated with a story picture to commemorate an anniversary or record a special event in a family history. In Germany, men used personalized shaving mugs that have become collectors' items.

Various methods have been worked out for adding a decoration to pottery, and many of the very ancient ones are still in vogue today. We cannot take the space to describe the techniques of glazing or how to fire a kiln, but on the following pages we will describe a number of ways to apply a design.

Figure 16. Earthen Pot with Slip Design.

Colored Slip. This is an ancient method of decorating a clay pot with colored slip. Slip is clay thinned with water until it has the consistency of heavy cream, and another ingredient must be added to give it color. This is done when the slip is first made by adding one of the oxides a little at a time to get the tone you want. The three oxides usually used are Iron for yellow, Cobalt for blue and Manganese for brown. The slip is painted onto the wet pot as soon as the walls are dry enough to take the pressure of the brush.

Another method is to allow the slip to partially dry and then remove motifs and lines with a sharp instrument.

Figure 17 shows a plate decorated with a process known as *"feathering."* It is done by first dipping the plate into thin colored slip and then adding a heavy top coat in another color. A feather or sharp pointed instrument is used to draw in fine lines.

Figure 17. Plate with Feather Decoration.

Figure 18. Underglaze Designs on Pitchers.

This process of decoration is different from the others in that the pot must be fired once before the design is applied. Underglazes come in a large range of colors and are mixed in water until they are the consistency of heavy cream. The design is then painted onto the pot with a small brush and allowed to dry. It is then dipped into a clear glaze and fired.

Figure 18 shows underglaze decorations on pitchers. Note that each pitcher was divided into a number of areas before the design was applied.

Figure 19. Early Underglazed Pottery Pieces.

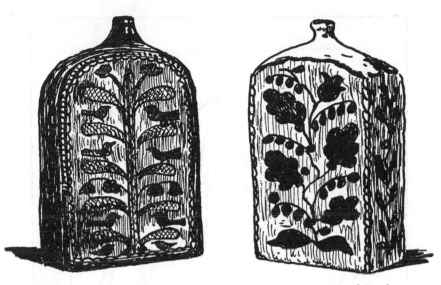

Figure 20. Modeled Design.   **Figure 21. Incised Design.**

Here are typical examples of early pottery made in central Europe. The thick walls and squat forms of the vessels give them a certain charm. The same motif is used to decorate each piece, but the sequence in different.

Modeled Designs are ones that have extra clay added to make them stand up in relief from the background. This type of decoration must be applied as soon as the pot is made, or before the clay becomes dry. Model the motifs and ridges from small pellets of clay and press them into the wall and seal in place with slip. Be sure to have all ridges in equal thickness and keep them in low relief.

Incised Designs. The bottle in Figure 21 shows a typical design done in low relief. This method of decoration is best used on slab pottery where the cuts are made before the walls are sealed together. The pattern is made up of lines cut out of the clay by using a blunt instrument. The lines should be of equal depth and as little crossing as possible. The glaze will run into the incisions when fired, thus filling them.

Figure 22. Inlaid Tile.

Inlaid design is an ancient method of decorating tiles for floors because the design wore away and not off with wear and tear of feet. However, this type of decoration is suitable for other tiles, particularly if the motif is large and of a solid color as the one shown in Figure 22.

To inlay a design, fill the tile box with clay and then trace a design on top. Cut down about ¼" all around the outline then remove the center by gouging it out. Now pour in enough colored slip to have it come up even with the surface, or push in some clay of another color. Even off the surface by passing a ruler over it.

Figure 23. Salt Glazed Jar.

Salt Glaze was used on so much of the old pottery, we just want to describe how it was done. This method of glazing is not to be attempted by an amateur. It is used by pottery firms that have chimneys for carrying away the smoke and fumes. The clay pots are dried and packed into the kiln as for bisquing and at a high temperature salt is thrown onto the fire. The salt vapour combines with the silica and alumina in the clay to form a beautiful transparent wall. The decoration usually stands out in relief.

Earthenware is a type of pottery that is made from a second-rate clay that has not been well refined. It is more porous and not suitable for detailed work. Figure 24 shows a typical earthenware dish.

Figure 24. Hungarian Earthenware Dish.

Figure 25. Mexican Pottery.

We are more or less familiar with Mexican pottery in the United States, but these examples are illustrated as a contrast to the European forms and designs in the chapter. Note that the shapes are similar but the subjects of designs entirely different.

Figure 26. Pottery Cupboard.

If you want to add a folk note to your dining room, why not construct a pottery cupboard. The one illustrated above is built on a simple plan with four shelves held in place with a series of slats. The decorative pieces at the top and bottom are cut from half inch pine or three-ply wood. The charm is added by displaying pieces of colorful peasant pottery not only on the shelves, but from small hooks screwed around the edges of the cupboard.

Hungarian Gate.　　　　　　　**Garden Shrine.**

To the peasant, flowers are a necessity of life and a little garden belongs in front of the house. None can go to church without a flower and the choicest ones are placed in the hands of friends as a token of friendship or hospitality. The yard is enclosed by a fence and the Hungarians work with loving skill to paint, chisel or carve a gate worthy of an entrance to their home. Great significance is vested in the gate for the moment a person opens it and passes through, he becomes a guest of the house and is welcomed before entering the door. On many were inscribed greetings such as:

> "Wanderer! This gate is not to bar the way—
> It shows you where to enter night and day."

The frames of the old gates were elaborately carved as shown in the above illustration. At the top was usually a dove cote, also a symbol of hospitality as it served as a shelter for the birds.

A shrine with a religious figure was often placed near the gate for the benefit of the passerby. However, the box was sometimes used for displaying treasures or a doll without religious significance. They also held tokens to ward off evil spirits.

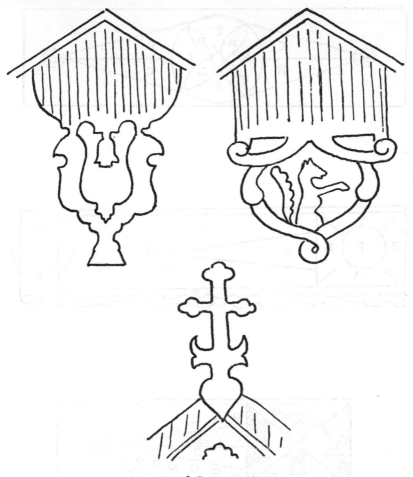

Roof Ornaments.

Designs, such as the ones above, are cut from wood and placed at the peak of the roof. They are found in Switzerland, particularly in the Tyrol region, where they seem to blend with the architecture of the chalets and cottages. The ornaments used for decoration were usually placed just under the peak of the roof but if the design includes a cross, as the one shown above, it always stood above the house and against the sky. This particular ornament was painted red, but usually they were left in the natural wood or painted in the same color as the house or trim.

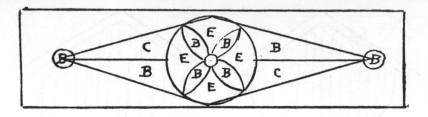

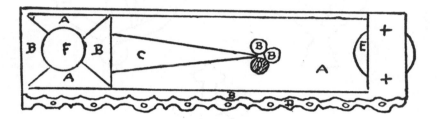

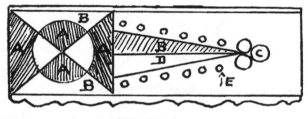

Hex Signs.

These colorful designs originated in the Tyrol country and other parts of Central Europe. They are painted in bold colors to frighten away evil spirits and to protect the building. In this country we find them on the barns of the Pennsylvania Dutch farmers where they were painted to "hex" anyone that might mar their contents. Here are three authentic signs with a key to their colors:

A. Gray	D. Yellow
B. Red	E. White
C. Green	F. Black

Window Shutters.

Window shutters are an important part of any house in Central Europe as a protection against cold and heavy snows. They are made from a solid piece of wood without ventilating slats as we have in this country. If you will search in books on European architecture, you will find some of the finest and most interesting folk art designs on the doors and around the windows of the peasant cottages. The window shutters illustrated above show two types—one a rectangle that closes together and the other—a decorative type with scalloped edges. The designs are painted with oil paints and varnished.

73

Porch Railings.

The Swiss chalets and cottages in the mountain regions have their windows, porches and doors decorated in folk designs and the gay colors make them most inviting. Sometimes, too, the most elaborate fret work is used around the eaves of the roofs, balconies and trim for the porches. We have selected a few of the simple ideas that an unskilled craftsman can make for his cottage or home if he wishes to add a bit of folk flavor.

The designs shown above are simple, yet very folk-like, balcony or porch railings cut out of one-half-inch pine. Note that one half of the design is cut from each of two boards so that they are placed together to complete the motif. Usually, if the designer was creative, each panel was different yet tied together by similarity of motif and size. If you want a more colorful railing, just paint the design instead of cutting it out with a saw.

This same fret work was used to decorate panels for fences and garden gates. The designs above were taken from a porch railing in Austria.

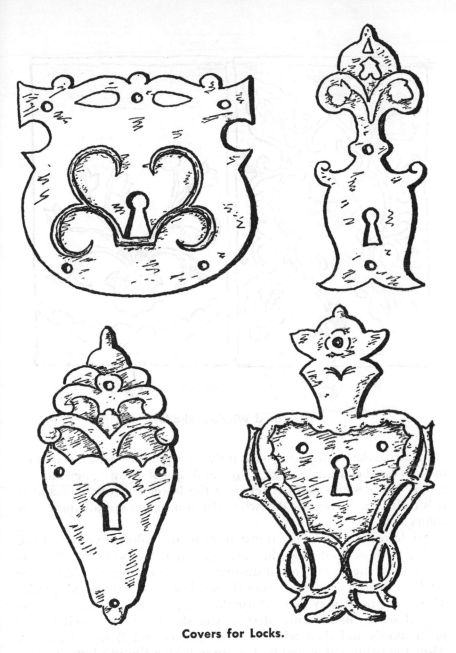

Covers for Locks.

Among interesting folk art designs are the iron covers for locks. They were wrought in the most elaborate patterns, particularly when very large keys were used. Here are a few of the more modern designs which can be made without too much skill on the part of the craftsman.

Decorated Window Shades.

In Switzerland and Northern Italy, the peasants paint elaborate designs on the window shades thus adding color and gaiety to the room. The design should cover only the lower half of the shade as it is rolled up during the day when the sun brings out all the lovely colors.

To decorate a shade, use transparent textile colors if you want the design to show up during the day. Opaque colors will only show at night when the room is not illuminated, or on the reverse side of the shade so that it can be seen from the yard or street. Any good quality of tempera paint may be used for this purpose. If you want to paint several shades in the same design, you should cut a stencil of the main motifs and then add connecting lines and flowers by hand. After the paint is thoroughly dry, spray with a liquid plastic to protect the design.

Figure 1. Peruvian Pottery.

The decoration on the above pieces of pottery and gourds on the opposite page, make an interesting contrast to those found in Europe and Asia. The decoration of gourds in South America is a well known craft and many of the designs are outstanding enough to be shown in a museum.

To Decorate Gourds, the first step is to dry them carefully in a cool place. Be sure there is no break or cut in the skin which would allow bacteria to enter during the drying process. After the gourd is dry, the top is cut off and seeds removed. The design is applied by cutting into the background with small veining gouges as in cutting a block print. A burning instrument can also be used. Figure 2 shows two gourds decorated by Peruvians.

Figure 2. Gourds, Peru.

Figure 1. Tin Mask and Candle Holder.

The Mexicans have made the most of tin as a craft medium and some of their projects rank high in the field of craftsmanship. It is easy to cut, and the tools required to mold it are so few almost anyone can practice tincraft. Tin is the most inexpensive metal on the market, yet it has a primitive quality that in some ways makes it more pleasing than brass or copper.

To work with tin, you will need a good pair of curved tin shears, a pair of pliers and a set of files. Some wooden molds are also useful for shaping a project. The individual pieces are fastened together with soft solder, so if you want to work with tin to this extent, you should buy a soldering iron.

Figure 1 shows two favorite Mexican craft objects—a mask and candle holder.

Figure 2. A basket made of one large box and two small ones. Make the large one of wood and the two small ones of tin. The handles both open and close the box.

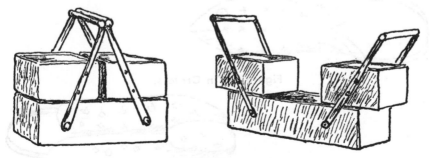

Figure 2. Mexican Box-basket.

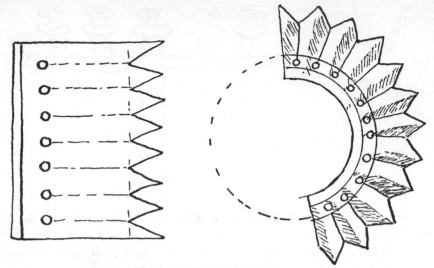

Figure 3. Tin Mirror Frame.

A technique often used with tin for a decoration is to bend it into accordion-like pleats as shown in Figure 3. Sometimes the edge is notched as it is in the mirror frame, or it can be left with a straight edge. Small holes are drilled along the inside edge through which a fine wire is threaded to gather the pleats together to form a circle. A plain, decorated circular band of tin about three-quarter-inch wide is placed on top of the pleats next to the edge of the mirror.

Tin Graters are made in many interesting forms. Here are two natural designs—a fish and a cactus. Cut out the design from a piece of heavy tin and drive a nail through from the back to make a series of rough holes that can be used for grating the rind of an orange or lemon. Round the edges by bending them back over a wire that becomes a frame as well as a handle at the top.

Figure 4. Tin Graters.

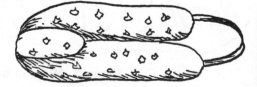

Figure 5. Tin Plates.

Plates, dishes or trays are usually decorated with metal background stamps or chasing tools. Cut the disc or oval out of tin, apply the design and then shape it in a mold. First, select your background stamps and consider various motifs, trying to visualize the kind of decoration they will make when repeated a number of times. Press in the design by holding the stamp upright and striking with a hammer. The lines are put in with a chasing tool.

If you want to make a large tray such as the one illustrated in Figure 6, you must reinforce it with wood. Either make a wood rim or make the whole foundation of wood or heavy metal.

Figure 6. Tin Tray.

Figure 7. Decorated Tin.

Adding Color to Tin is done by first cleaning the surface thoroughly with fine steel wool. The decoration is much more effective if the motifs only are painted and the background allowed to remain in the natural tin. Use the usual lacquer that is manufactured for painting metal. These paints come in very bright shiny colors which surprisingly lose their gaudiness when applied to this type of craft. This is a decoration that fits well into a modern setting.

The rooster illustrated in Figure 8 is made by first making a body of tin then cutting the feathers separate and soldering them in place with soft solder.

Figure 8. Tin Rooster.

Candle Sticks

Here are examples of wooden candle sticks decorated with colorful folk designs. While they look very ornate, the construction is simple lathe and saw work. The painting gives the richness in design.

The little Pine tree shown above is a Swedish design. Notice that the tree is cut from two pieces of wood, with a slit cut in either end. By sliding one down over the other, it forms a four-sided tree.

Sampler

This type wall decoration varied from one of exquisite design to a simple alphabet done by a child. They were often used for practice in making stitches—hence the name. The oldest ones were embroidered on coarse linen, but later a loosely woven canvas or net was used for the background. If you want to make a sampler, sketch out a design on graph paper. The outline of the motifs should be in tiny squares as it will be embroidered with cross stitches. Such motifs as houses, trees, flowers or people are usually used. Turn to the chapter on embroidery for instructions on how to make a cross stitch.

3. Crafts For Personal Adornment

THE FOLK ARTS reach their highest peak when it comes to personal adornment. From prehistoric times to the present day, people have created things to enhance their personal appearance. This is true of men as well as women among the peasants, for the male adorned himself in almost as colorful garb as the women by adding embroidery to his garment and gay feathers to his hat. The peasant women spend hours embroidering their costumes and one dress will last a lifetime because it is worn only on state occasions. Many of the devices used by women today to enhance their dress were denied the peasant for lack of materials and tools. However, many unbelievably beautiful pieces of jewelry and leather items were made with crude home-made tools and the designs were superb. We have selected some of the most representative examples of this type and ones that will blend with our modern dress to describe on the following pages.

Leathercraft

Leather is one of the most popular craft media in the creative field today. It is enjoyed by both men and women and there are many techniques that can be accomplished by children. Since there are many excellent books in public libraries on the subject of leathercraft, we are going to explain some of the primitive methods of decorating leather with a few handmade tools.

This craft varied in different countries according to the type of leather that was available and the usefulness of the project. For instance, in the Near East camel hide and goat skin are the popular hides as well as sheep skin. In Middle Europe, we find pigskin, cowhide, goatskin and sheepskin. The northern countries, such as Finland, Norway and Sweden, had an abundance of doeskin which was also used for clothing. Since cowhide lends itself to tooling, some of the most interesting examples of leathercraft are to be found in Hungary, France, Bulgaria and Germany.

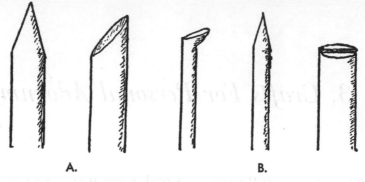

A.   **B.**

Figure 1. Wooden Leather Tools.

The projects made by the folk people have a charm all their own, partly because of the simplicity of design and also because they are purely functional. A great deal of personality was transferred by the maker as the main motifs usually told a story of his profession or pastimes such as hunting, tending the flocks, his home, etc. They were applied to the leather with simple, handmade tools such as the ones shown in Figure 1.

Figure 1A shows two necessary tools, a tracer and modeler that can be made from a one-quarter-inch dowel. A tracer is made by sharpening one end to a fine point and a modeler is cut on a slant for pushing down the background. Smaller tools can be made from a one-eighth-inch dowel and Figure 1B suggests useful shapes.

Another means of decorating leather is to press down the background with a stamp of something. They are made with various outlines as shown in Figure 2. This is a favorite technique in Mexico where the stamps are also used to decorate metal. To make a set of wooden stamps file away the background until the motif stands about one-eighth-inch in relief as shown in the illustration. Wet the leather, place the stamp in place and hit it with a wooden mallet.

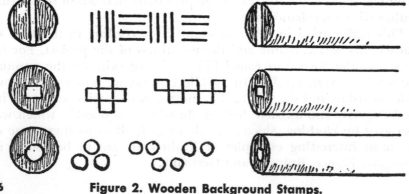

Figure 2. Wooden Background Stamps.

Figure 3. Hungarian Purse Design.

How to Decorate Leather

Almost every technique was used for applying a design, tooling, applique, stamping or burning on the decoration with a hot instrument. The Hungarians used inlays of various color leathers to develop their folk designs. This was accomplished as follows:

To Inlay a Design. Select two pieces of leather of contrasting color and lay one on top of the other. Trace design on the top piece and cut out the motif with a sharp knife, being sure to cut through both pieces of leather at the same time. Cement the top piece to a piece of skiver (split leather) and then fill in the holes with motifs cut from the other piece. Connect the design by tooling lines and curves.

Burning Leather. Use steel knitting needles for this process. Heat them over a flame and follow the same directions as for burning wood.

Tooling Leather. Dampen the leather and transfer the design by laying it on top and pressing it down with a tracer. If you want to press the design into the background as shown in Figure 3, go over the lines again with a tracing tool. Another treatment is to press down the background with a spoon modeler and bring the design up in relief as in Figure 4.

Figure 4. Swedish Belt Design.

Figure 5. Lapland Match Boxes.

Match Boxes

Match boxes have been an important accessory to the peasant since matches were invented and we find beautiful examples of ones made from leather and wood. They fulfill a two-fold purpose, one to keep the matches dry and the other to keep them together in one place. Here are two interesting boxes made in Lapland; notice that the lids are attached to a cord which in turn is tied to the box to keep it from being lost. Both of these covers can be made to fit over a small match box and the emery placed at the bottom for striking.

We selected a match cover from Hungary because of its interesting design. It can also be used for a cigarette cover if you prefer.

Figure 6. Hungarian Match Cover.

Figure 7. Leather Suspenders.

Suspenders, such as the one shown above, were worn with leather breeches. In the Tyrol, they are sometimes combined with felt or other materials and then decorated in gay peasant designs. The buttonholes at the front are attached to a piece of elastic which is then fastened to the suspenders about three inches from the bottom. This gives the suspenders the necessary stretch and at the same time holds them tightly in place at the shoulders. It is best to use calfskin for tooling a design and then line the straps with a thin leather. If you wish to carve the design, use cowhide but leave the straps unlined.

Figure 8. African Leather Designs.

We have selected these as an interesting contrast to the other designs and projects described in this chapter.

Figure 9. Purse and Slipper with Mosaic Designs.

Mosaic Designs in Leather

This method of decoration is excellent for use on non-tooling leather when a design of some kind is desired. It is used in Egypt and the Near East where most of the hides cannot be tooled, but where there is an abundance of leather. The bag in Figure 9 is made with blond colored leather and laced with white.

To decorate in mosaics plan a design that can be woven in and out alternately on succeeding rows, see Figure 10. Punch the holes with a leather slitting tool (they come with one, four or eight prongs). You will need the dingle prong for turning corners. Use goatskin lacing in various colors for the mosaics and draw it in and out the slits with a lacing needle. Allow the lacing to extend one-quarter-inch beyond the first and last hole and cement in place with rubber cement.

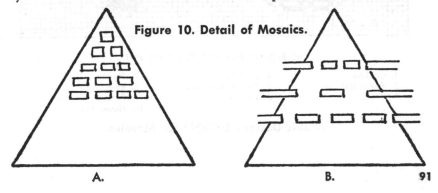

Figure 10. Detail of Mosaics.

A.

B.

THE FLOWER POT AND THE KOHL POT

1. Cauliflower.
2. Key of Hebron.
3. Cock.

4. Kohl Pot.
5. Four Eggs in a Pan.
6. Ladder.

7. Pigeon.
8. Rainbow.
9. Foreign Rainbow.
10. Flower Pot.

Arabic Designs Suitable for Mosaics.

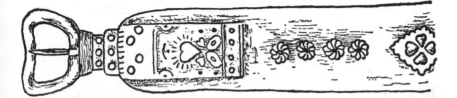

Figure 11. Italian Belts.

The three belts illustrated above are made of felt and decorated with pieces of leather. The leather parts are cut from calfskin and decorated before being attached to the material either by cement or sewing with a saddle stitch. Large strips of leather should be held in place by sewing, but small medallions or motifs will adhere with a coat of rubber cement.

This style belt can be enhanced by adding bits of decorated metal either on the leather or on the belt itself. Some thought should be given also to the design of the buckle—these are interesting belts, so an ornate buckle should add to their charm. The buckles illustrated in Figure 12 might be appropriate. They can be made of metal and the design etched, or the decoration can be tooled in calfskin and glued onto a metal or wood base.

Figure 12. Belt Buckles.

These are typical belt buckles worn on folk costumes. They can be made of leather, metal or wood.

Figure 13. Purse from French Morocco.

How to Add Color to Leather

1. Appliqued Designs. Cut motifs from varied color leathers and glue onto a neutral colored background with rubber cement. After the small pieces are cut and cemented in place, dampen the edges and smooth with a leather tool. You can buy scrap leather in assorted colors by the pound and they are excellent for use in working out a folk design.

2. India Ink is used when bright, vivid colors are required in a design. You can buy this ink in assorted colors at any stationery store. Apply with a soft brush.

3. Water Color or Oils are used for adding more subtle colors. Use oil paints for shading of different tones.

The French Morocco purse and Mexican coasters are decorated in vivid colors typical of the countries. The designs are brought into relief by tooling before the color is added.

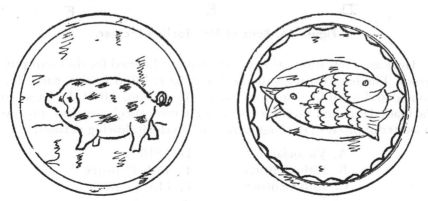

Figure 14. Mexican Coasters.

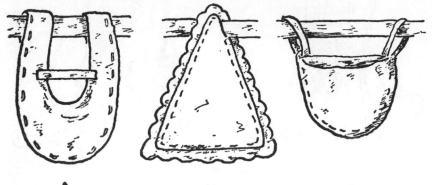

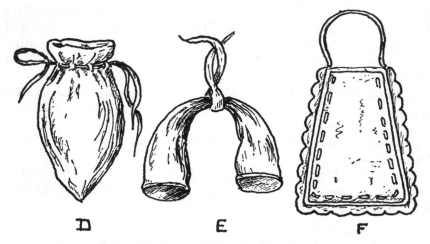

Figure 15. Bags of Non-Tooling Leather.

Here are a few interesting purses that can be used for different purposes. The bags worn on the belts can be reduced in size, gaily decorated and worn by women as a dress decoration. All of the bags can be made large and used for collecting nature specimens in camp. As a matter of interest, the bags were worn in the following periods:

A. Victorian
B. 16th Century
C. 15th Century

D. 1810
E. 15th Century
F. 14th Century

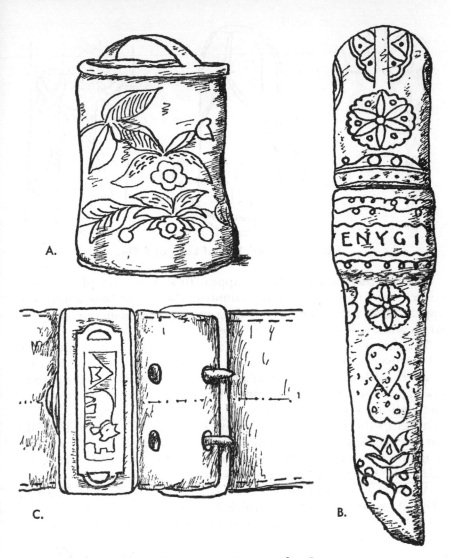

A.

C.

B.

Figure 16. Leather Projects for Camp.

A. **Utility Bag.** The entire bag can be made of leather, or you can make a canvas bag and add a leather front. This type of bag can be made in any style but keep pleasing proportions.

B. **Knife Sheath.** This is a small sheath designed to cover a knife that is to be carried in the pocket. Make the lid a little larger so it will fit down over the handle of the knife.

C. **Buckle.** This design is added because it is interesting. It was originally used on the girth of a saddle.

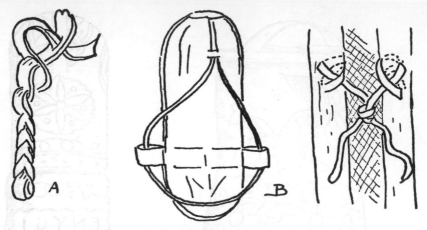

Figure 1. Detail Sandal Lace and Tie.

Since leather sandals have an appeal to so many people, we have collected examples from various countries that might have a universal appeal. They are all made according to the same principle, only the straps and methods of tying are different.

You will need three types of leather—a piece of cowhide for top of sole, calfskin for the straps and heavy sole leather for the bottom. Draw an outline of each foot on a piece of paper and make the pattern one-eighth-inch larger all around. Trace this on a piece of cowhide and indicate on it the position of the straps you have selected in relation to the toes. Next cut straps and thread them through slits cut in cowhide sole. Draw them through about one-half inch and glue to the back as shown in B. After straps are adjusted and in place, sew this to the heavy sole leather with a saddle stitch.

A. shows how to make a leather lacing by threading two narrow strips of leather through slits which are cut as you go along.

C. Method of tying sandal to foot by adjusting the tie at the toes.

D. Detail of undersole.

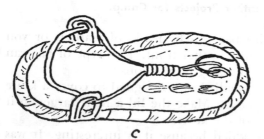

Figure 2. Detail of Sandal Tie and Undersole.

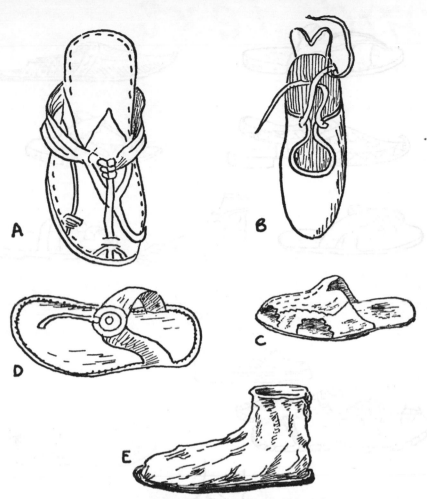

Figure 3. Sandals from Various Countries.

A. **India.** This sandal is fitted to the foot by two straps and there is one around the big toe.

B. **Lapland.** A moccasin made of doeskin and lined with fur. It is designed for walking in the snow.

C. **England.** This mule-like sandal can be made with straps of elastic with a piece of leather sewed to the front to keep them together.

D. **Africa.** Most common type of sandal with strap between toes to hold it to the foot.

E. **Japan.** This shoe is made from cloth sewed onto a heavy sole. Gussets are sewed in around the ankles to make it fit the foot.

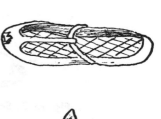

Figure 4. Sandal Designs.

Here are interesting sandals from different countries in Europe and Asia. They show different types of straps and lacings that can be easily copied by looking at the picture.

100

Embroidery

Embroidery has been woman's art through the ages—how long can only be surmised. As time progressed, exquisite stitching was added to the garments to express a love for the beautiful. Just as an artist transfers his ideas to a canvas, so the folk women created beautiful designs in simple lines and bright, vivid colors.

The decoration of a peasant dress tells a story of the homeland. Every country has developed its own intricate stitches of simple and advanced embroidery. The colors employed in a design are also distinctive as they were always made from natural dyes found nearby. However, variation in embroidery is an accumulation of the ages so that today we find the same basic designs on all peasant dresses.

Many of the all-over embroidered designs give the impression of being so intricate that they could not possibly have been created by human hands. However, they are in truth basically simple. A close analysis will show that the same steps are repeated over and over again until they are blended into a whole and tied together with many colors. The design is a play of straight and curved lines that join together larger motifs such as flowers, birds, animals, etc.

If you want to use folk motifs for embroidery, it is best to go to the library for authentic designs. They are absolutely correct for stitches and the design cannot be improved. At the moment we suffer from designs made by artists who understand drawing as applied to line and water color, but have no knowledge of the stitches required to execute a flower. Keep your designs simple and enhance them by adding bright colors.

Since an embroidered design is made up of motifs connected by straight and curved lines, we have selected the most useful techniques for giving instruction. Select the motif you want (flowers, leaves, hearts, etc.), place them on the object you wish to decorate, then join them with one of the line stitches described on the following page.

101

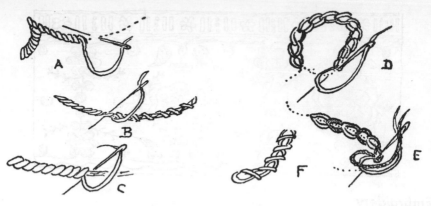

Figure 1. Line Stitches.

A. Outline or Stem Stitch. This stitch is the one most commonly used in all embroideries. Take a short slanting stitch from right to left and bring needle out to left at end of first stitch. Always keep the thread below the needle. If you want a thicker line, use the *Whipped Stem Stitch,* Figure 1B, or *Raised Stem Stitch,* Figure 1C. You will be able to make these stitches by following the drawings.

D. Chain Stitch. This stitch is made by bringing needle up through cloth, holding thumb over loop of thread and inserting needle near place it first came up as shown in the drawing. Where the point of needle comes out determines size of loop. The *Double Chain Stitch,* Figure 1E, is employed when two colors are used. A *Whipped Chain Stitch,* Figure 1F, is used for thick stems and the crosses can be made of a contrasting color.

Figure 2. Back Stitches.

Figure 2A. Take a small running stitch, reinsert the needle at the end of the stitch and bring it to the wrong side. Carry the thread to twice the length of the original stitch and bring needle up and back down at left of stitch as shown in the illustration. A *Threaded Back Stitch* is used for adding a second color.

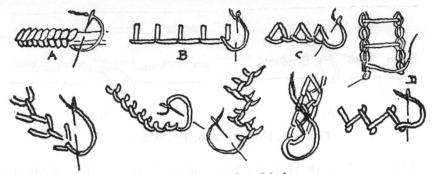

Figure 3. Decorative Stitches.

Figure 3A. Button Hole Stitch. This stitch is used to finish edges and outline areas.

Figure 3B. Blanket Stitch. Made in the same manner as button hole stitch only loops are farther apart.

Figure 3C. Closed Blanket Stitch. Pass needle through cloth slanting it from right to left and up through extreme edge of work as shown in the illustration. Slant second stitch in opposite direction to meet first stitch, thus closing them at top.

Figure 3D. Ladder Stitch. Make two rows of chain stitches (Fig. 1D) and pass a thread from one side to the other to form a ladder.

Figure 3 (bottom row). Feather Stitches. First take a slanting stitch on the right side of line pointing needle to the left and then point needle in opposite direction on next stitch.

Figure 4. French Knot and Lazy Daisy.

Figure 4A. French Knot. Tie a knot in end of thread and pull needle up from the back. Wrap the thread around needle several times, according to size knot you wish to make, and insert needle back into same hole. This stitch is used for making flowers.

Figure 4B. Lazy Daisy. Bring needle up in center of flower and hold thumb over loop and then insert needle as close as possible to the hole where the thread came out. Now take a long stitch underneath and come out at lower part of petal.

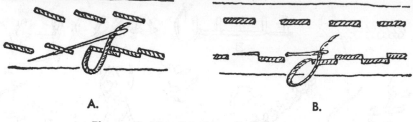

A.   B.

Figure 5. Line Stitch or Holbein Stitch.

Figure 5. Line or Holbein Stitch. This is the simplest of all embroidery stitches and can be undertaken by those who have little or no experience. It is often combined with the cross stitch in trimming corners or for outlining a design. In order to work this stitch, it is necessary to make two journeys. The first journey is around the outline of the design, making each stitch and space between equally the same in length. Now turn the work around and fill in the spaces between the stitches on the journey back. Insert the needle *above* stitch on right side and out *below* left side of stitch as shown in Figure 5A. Do not make stitches as shown in Figure 5B as the line will not be straight. If the embroidery is to be done in two colors, the inner part should be in the lighter one and the outer borders in the darker one.

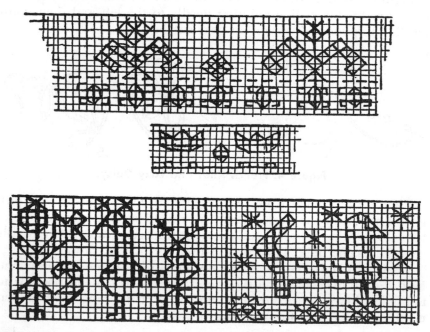

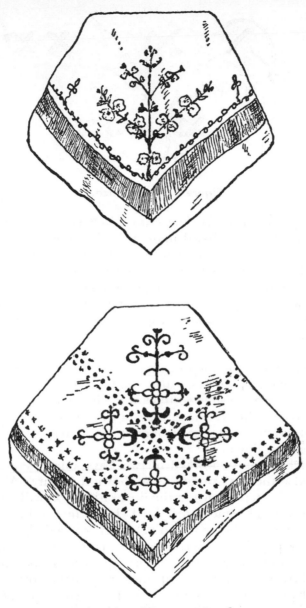

Embroidered Peasant Scarfs.

These scarfs are made of thin wool and decorated with silk floss.
The designs are made by using a combination of the stem stitch, running stitch and the Holbein stitch. The above examples show two
methods of dividing an area.

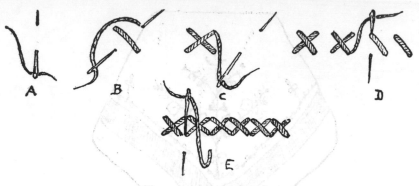

Figure 6. Cross Stitch.

Next to line embroidery, the cross stitch is the simplest of the decorative stitches. It is based upon a stitch made in the form of a cross and its beauty depends upon the uniformity of the stitches. The designs and color combinations are universal but the best examples come from central Europe—Rumania, Hungary, Bulgaria and Jugoslavia, etc., where the peasants have decorated their clothes and household linens for centuries. The European peasants work out their own designs by counting threads and without the guide of either a graph or transfer.

Cross stitches may be used to decorate almost any article such as toweling, table linen, blouses, scarfs, etc. Be sure to choose a material of an even weave as an uneven thickness will completely change the pattern. Choose a thread comparable in thickness to those woven in the background material. Use wool on heavy, coarse cloth and a mercerized cotton on linen.

Cross stitches may be worked in two ways—one where each cross is completed as the work progresses as shown in Figure 6A, B, and C. By following the steps shown in the illustration, you will see how this is accomplished. This method is used chiefly in turning corners or where only a few crosses are required to carry out a design. Figure 6D and E show a popular method of making cross stitches when a long straight row of crosses are included in a pattern. In the first row of single stitches, bring needle up at lower right hand corner, down at upper left hand corner and repeat until row is completed. On return journey, bring needle up at lower left hand corner and down at upper right hand corner. In working the stitches, always work across the row from right to left forming the first slanting stitches and then work from left to right to complete the stitch. Add a second row in the same manner as shown in Figure 6E. Note that the needle is thrust into the same hole as was used to make lower part of cross.

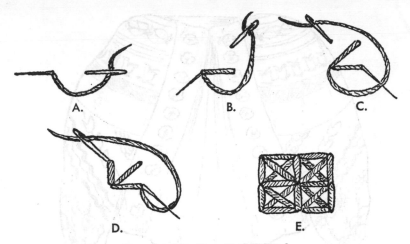

Figure 7. Italian Cross Stitch.

In order to work this stitch, the design must include two parallel rows of crosses. You can carry out two solid rows of stitches at a time by repeating the squares. You may also want to use this method for turning corners or making individual squares. First, mark off a square by counting threads and indicating the four corners. Study the steps given in the above illustration and begin by making a horizontal stitch from left to right as shown in A. Next, carry the thread diagonally across and make a slant stitch B. Now carry the thread away from center and make a slant stitch as shown in C. Continue as shown in D and E until the cross is formed.

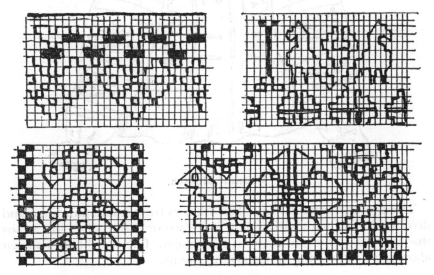

Cross Stitch Designs.

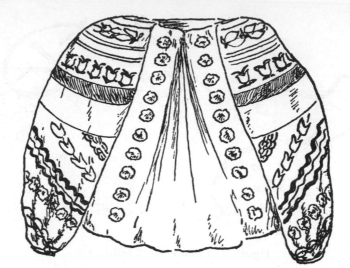

Peasant Blouses.

The peasants usually made their blouses from homespun linen and decorated them with various stitches. Two or three colors in various shades were carried throughout the design. The two blouses shown above have interesting design arrangements.

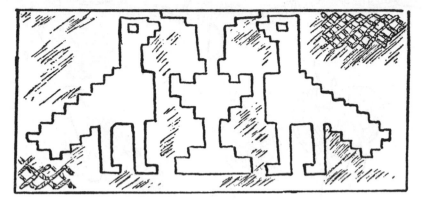

Figure 8. Assi Embroidery.

This type of embroidery is just opposite to the cross stitch in that the design is left bare and the background decorated with crosses. It is derived from the ancient Italian embroidery and gives great dignity to the work as the designs are heraldic in character and are used on altar cloths, banners, etc.

The designs are first worked out on graph paper and then transferred onto the material. Count the threads as you transfer the design to be sure it is entirely straight with the material. Before putting the background crosses in, outline the whole design with the Holbein or double running stitch as shown in Figure 5A. Be sure to make each running stitch the same length as the crosses. The stitches should extend over three threads in the material. The cross stitches are made by first making a row of diagonal stitches and then going back to complete them. There will be gaps in the background between the cross stitches and the outline of the design which spoils the appearance of the work. Fill these in with small slanting stitches so that the design will be completely framed.

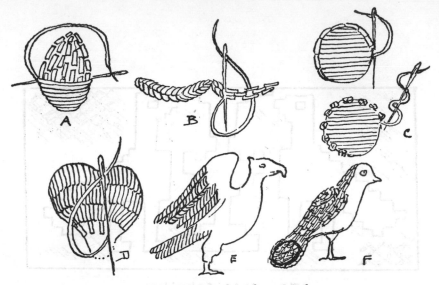

Figure 9. Solid Embroidery Stitches.

Solid embroidery is used for making the important motifs in a design and silk, cotton or gold threads may be used in this technique. The usual method is to first outline the design with small running stitches, and then pad the center with closely placed rows of outline stitches to bring it up in relief. Be sure to use thread or floss in a matching color, but if you are using a fine strand to cover the top it is well to use a coarse thread for the padding. Cover the design with close, even stitches by going over and over again with the thread as shown in Figure 9A. If you are making scallops, pad them in the same manner and cover the padding with a close blanket or button hole stitch, Figure 9B.

Figure 9C shows two methods of outlining a circle after it is embroidered. It is very difficult to make a perfectly round circle with stitches, so place a row of back stitches or french knots around the outer rim. These circles are used primarily for centers of flowers.

Figure 9D illustrates a method of filling in large areas by using a series of long and short stitches. This method is used in conjunction with solid embroidery very often to lighten the design.

Figure 9E shows how large areas can be broken up into a series of small ones as in the wings and tail of the eagle. They are placed parallel and as close together as possible.

Figure 9F shows how sometimes the motif is outlined with desired color, and the detail or features outlined in a contrasting color. The whole center is filled in with rows of small chain stitches.

110

Peasant Motifs in Embroidery.

These are some of the important motifs used in embroidery. Use them by scattering them throughout the design and connect together with lines and curves. Be sure to keep a balance by selecting subjects of equal weight and size and repeat the same colors on either end. These motifs can be simply outlined, or you may fill in the center according to methods suggested in Figure 9.

Flower Patterns for Embroidery.

Flowers are a favorite motif for all types of embroidery. They are decorative and are used for adding color and they can be adapted to any shape or size in a design. There are many ways of making a flower but the above examples are given because they are adapted to the various embroidery stitches. Try to avoid making a flower realistic as much as possible.

Leaf Patterns for Embroidery.

Leaves should be as inconspicuous as possible so that they will blend into the background of a design. Just as the stems join the motifs with straight and simple lines, so the leaves soften the bright colors and bring harmony to the finished work. Notice that some of the leaves are simply outlined with veins indicated with simple stitches. Others have a portion of the surface in solid embroidery, while the other portion is in chain or stem stitch.

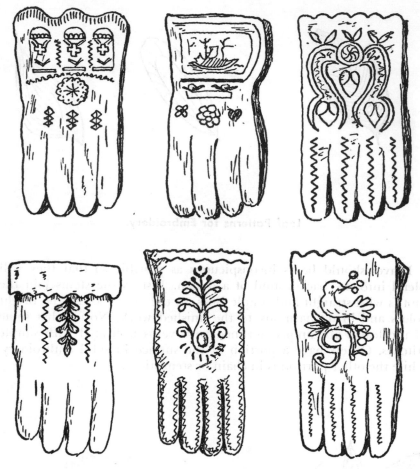

Gloves—Embroidery Designs.

These gloves come from Norway and are embroidered in native designs. Any glove material such a doeskin, felt or wools can be used. If you wish to decorate the fingers or upper part of the hand, be sure to do the embroidery before stitching the parts of the glove together. It is also possible to buy a pair of gloves in a department store, add embroidery stitches and line them if desired.

114

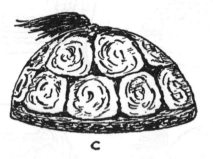

Peasant Caps—Boys'.

Here are three styles of boys' caps which are worn in rural communities or with native costumes. Make them with felt and embroider them with mercerized cotton thread. If you want to use a thinner material, decorate the parts and add a lining as you sew them together. The caps come from the following countries: A—Turkey, B—Romania and C—Dalmatia.

Peasant Caps—Girls'.

A peasant cap, or bonnet, is one of the distinguishing parts of a peasant costume. We have selected a few to show the different styles and how they are decorated. They are usually made of homespun linen or wool and embroidered with rows of bright colors with various motifs added for interest. Many colors of ribbons are added for ties or streamers.

Peasant Jacket.

These jackets are worn particularly in the Tyrol and the Swiss Alps. They are straight jackets that meet in front without buttons and are waist length or sometimes shorter. They are usually elaborately decorated with gay embroidery in designs such as shown above.

Tyrol Wool Designs.

These authentic designs can be used for decorating scarfs, mittens, jackets, belts, etc. Other materials such as mercerized cotton may also be used for embroidering linen or cotton materials.

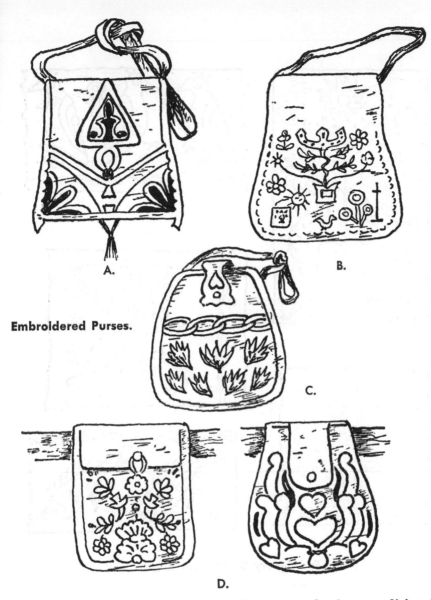

Embroidered Purses.

A.

B.

C.

D.

The long handled purses or bags in vogue today have traditionally been used by the peasants; however, not by women but by men. Here are a few typical designs that can be made from deer skin, felt or wool. Add a decoration of embroidered stitches in a thread comparable to the background material. A—is a bag from Norway. Notice the interesting catch or fastener. B—Lithuanian design that can also be used for beads. C—Design embroidered with gold cord couched onto background of leather. D—Two bags worn on belt.

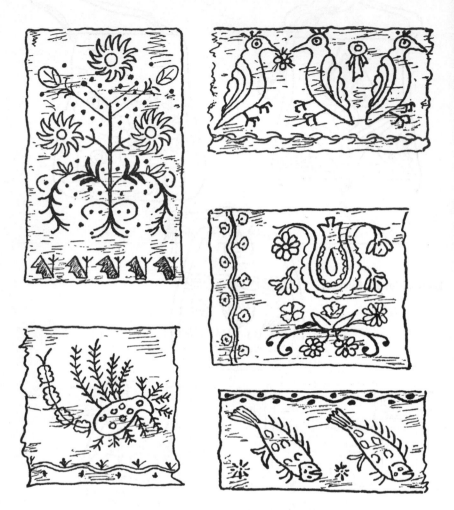

Embroidery Designs for Rugs.

These designs are especially suited for decorating rugs or wall hangings. If you do not wish to embroider them with rug wool, adapt them to canvas and hook the design with narrow strips of material.

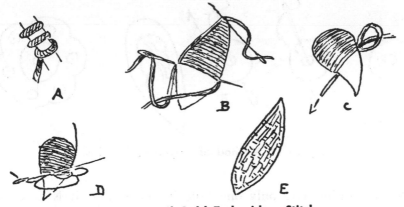

Figure 10. Detail Gold Embroidery Stitches.

For the working of this kind of embroidery, you will need gold and silver threads which can be bought in different thicknesses varying with the material you wish to decorate. This is used for solid embroidery. For outline work, or to make a design stand out, use a silk cord that comes in various sizes. It is necessary to use an embroidery hoop to hold material taut while working.

Figure 10A shows method of making stem by using silk cord, or a number of strands and holding in place with couching stitch.

Figure 10B. If your gold thread is heavy, use a stiletto or needle with a big eye for pulling thread through to under side. Figures C and D show two methods of making solid embroidery without carrying threads underneath. Use a second needle with thin thread in a matching color and fasten loops on either side.

Figure 10D shows method of using gold or silver purl for solid embroidery. Cut purl in exact lengths required in the design and sew in place as shown in drawing. Use thin thread in a matching color and fasten loops on either side as shown in illustration.

Figure 10E shows how a motif can be filled with rows of gold and silver cord held in place with couching stitches.

Designs Suitable for Gold Embroidery.

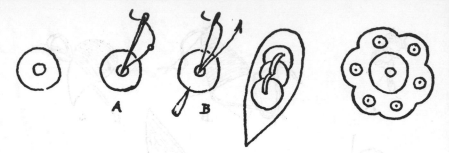

Figure 11. Method of Attaching Sequins.

Since sequins have only one hole in the center, it is necessary to sew a second object somewhat larger in the middle to keep it in place. The simplest method is to use a small glass bead that can be purchased at a ten cent or department store. Knot your thread and bring needle up at place you wish the sequin. Thread on sequin and then bead, push down over needle and push point back through the hole and pull taut. See Figure 11A. Another method is to buy gold or silver purl and cut into tiny pieces. Thread needle through center of purl and follow same directions as for bead as shown in Figure 11B. The drawing also illustrates how to sew sequins in a single row.

Flowers Embroidered with Gold and Sequins.

Oriental Capes.

These capes are worn by Egyptian women on dress occasions. The material in one cape is velvet, the other fine wool and both are lined is contrasting colors. Usually, a small cap in matching color and material is worn with the cape. A narrow border is embroidered in gold or silk threads and something in addition is usually added at the neck and shoulders. The combination of simplicity of design and rightness of material makes a beautiful cape.

Figure 1. Silver Earrings.

These are Egyptian and Greek designs that can be etched in silver for earrings or buttons. Most of the designs are different versions of the lotus flower, a favorite motif of the Egyptians. These designs are also suitable for carving in wood by removing the chips as indicated in Figure A.

Figure 2 shows two oriental designs suitable for clips or brooches. The design shown in the rectangle can be elongated for a bracelet.

Figure 2. Oriental Designs for Clip or Brooch.

Carved Buttons.

These heads dressed in native costume are carved from wood and used as buttons. Choose a wood that has a close grain such as bass or any of the hard woods. Since only the face stands out in relief, it is best to do the carving with a sharp knife. Add color by using water color or oil paint and cover the surface with a clear varnish. Insert small screw eyes in back for attaching the button to cloth. Since there are many projecting small points, these buttons should be used as a decorative device rather than holding two pieces of cloth together.

Figure 1. French Tole Buttons.

These French tole buttons have great charm if they are carefully made. The base is a disc cut from tin in any size and rounded in a wooden mold. Paint the background in any color you choose with colored lacquer or enamel and add designs with oils. Use some gold paint on the edges and a little here and there on the design itself. Make a small loop of wire and solder the ends on the back with soft solder for attaching button to a garment.

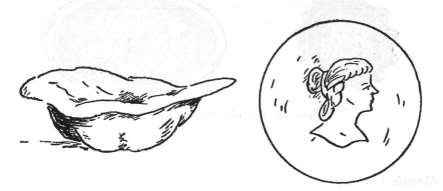

Figure 1. Cameo and Shell.

The making of cameos has long been one of Italy's most esteemed crafts, and these beautiful carvings are known and enjoyed throughout the world. Our text is too limited to go into its history, but we hope our few words on the subject will lead you to your library or, perhaps, encourage a little carving.

Cameos are carved from shells, the pink and brown from the large conch shell (Fig. 1), but other species are used if their walls have layers of various colors. If you examine a conch shell closely, you will see many small mounds of a white mineral deposit in contrast to the pink background. The craftsman selects the spots that have the deepest deposits and cuts these sections out of the shell with a jeweler's saw. The part that has the heaviest white is used for the head or design of the cameo. The natural contour of the shell gives just the right curve to the surface of the ornament.

The decoration is made by drawing an outline of the figure and then scraping away the white from around the edges, thus bringing the design up in relief against a pink background. Formerly, this work was accomplished with gouges and files, but today electric drills are used. This is not an impossible craft to pursue in a recreational craft program, yet it is not generally practiced. The traditional cameo head (woman with ancient hair-do) is by no means the only decoration used in Italy. The designs may depict landscapes, profiles of actual people or even a pet.

Figure 1. Mosaic Earring and Pin.

Mosaic Jewelry

Mosaic designs set in gold or silver bands are used in Italy and France for pins, bracelets, earrings, rings, etc. The tiny colored fragments that make up the design may be bits of enamel, glass or even precious stones. Most of the designs are naturalistic, such as flowers and leaves arranged to fit into the area of the pin.

The background of the ornament is cut from a piece of metal and the tiny mosaics cemented in place to develop a composition. If the enamel or stones are to be cut into tiny flowers, the pieces are sunk into a hardening surface so the craftsman can hold them in place while the cutting is done. The completed design is framed with a narrow band of gold or silver.

Florentine mosaics are distinguished from others found in Italy in that the design pieces are much larger and of a uniform size. The pieces are cut and inlaid into a background of onyx or malachite rather than building the entire surface of tiny pieces.

Figure 2. Florentine Mosaic.

4. Crafts for Camps and Playgrounds

A CAMPER should be interested in all the crafts described in this book because they are both primitive and functional—two qualities desired in a camp craft. However, we have selected some outdoor projects that are altogether suitable for a pioneer camp or living out of doors. Other crafts can be integrated with recreational activities such as dramatics, sports, nature, etc., for enriching programs in day camps or playgrounds. We believe the crafts of the shepherds are entirely new in this country and hope you will want to incorporate them in your camp programs. The following projects were selected at random with no thought of presenting them in a definite sequence or order.

Stump Stools

A stump, suitable for a stool, can be found in almost any woods and can be made quite functional by doing a little cutting in the right places. The shape of the finished stool will depend upon the quality of the stump and ability of the designer. In searching for a stump, keep an open mind as to shape or size and, above all, select one that will give you four sturdy legs and a comfortable seat. If you want your stool to resemble some sort of creature, just add the necessary features as shown in the illustration. You can add a more formal decoration by using a hammer and chisel to cut away the wood if the stump is in good condition.

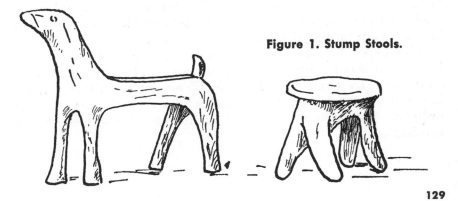

Figure 1. Stump Stools.

Figure 2. Muffin Rings.

We all eat English muffins, but how many have cooked their own on an iron griddle? The muffin itself is made from yeast dough that has been placed in a metal ring for cooking purposes. The ring serves a dual function—first, it holds the dough in shape and, second, it helps to retain heat as the muffin is being cooked. This type of muffin ring is an old-time craft, probably of English or Scottish origin.

For temporary muffin rings, you may make them of tin since it is easy to shape and always available in camp. However, if you like the idea of cooking bread on a griddle rather than an oven, you should use a heavier metal. Cut a strip 1″ x 12″ and fasten the ends together by over-lapping ½″ as shown in the illustration. Use soft solder or a rivet for the fastening.

To make the muffins, use a hot roll mix and follow the directions given on the box. Of course, you may get a recipe for yeast bread and make your own dough. The important thing to remember is that you allow the dough to rise *once,* then work it down and roll until it is ½″ in thickness. Use the muffin ring as a cutter and allow the dough to remain in the ring until it rises almost to the top of the brim. Now heat the griddle, grease it with shortening, and place muffins on to cook. It is necessary to keep the griddle at a low, even heat and keep turning the muffins as they cook.

It is also possible to use these metal rings for cooking corn muffins in the same manner. Place the rings at once on a hot griddle that has a little more fat than required for English muffins and fill them about half full of corn batter. Make the batter a little thicker than for ordinary corn muffins. Allow the mixture to rise and set before turning.

130

Figure 3. Barometer.

This is a traditional type of barometer made in Germany and Switzerland. It is constructed on the principle that a silk cord or violin string becomes shorter as it absorbs moisture from the air, and lengthens again as the humidity disappears.

The over-all shelter is a peasant cottage and at the front are two parallel doors as shown in the illustration. When the weather is about to change, a man stands in one door and a woman in the other; if the weather becomes clear and sunshiny the woman comes out on the porch; if it begins to rain, the woman goes back into the house and the man comes out. The figures are set on a small platform which is attached to a silk cord running perpendicularly from roof to floor of the house. As the twist in the cord shrinks, it turns the platform enough to make the man and woman do a half turn.

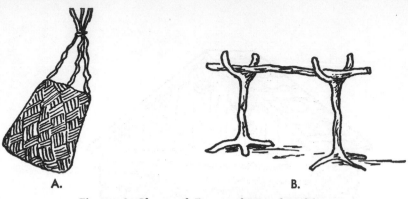

A.   B.

Figure 4. Charcoal Fan and Wood Holder.

Figure 4A. This is a fan made from raffia to keep embers burning in a charcoal fire. It is a type used in Mexico and is often woven in colorful designs, particularly for household use. A crude fan made of twigs and sedges will serve temporarily in camp.

Figure 4B. We add this idea just for interest because it might be adapted for use in a pioneer kitchen. The one illustrated above is the type used by Persians to hold wood fagots near a fire where dye pots are boiling.

A Primitive Laundry

A peasant spends many hours carving designs on a mangle and washing beetle for his bride. Figure 5 shows some of the interesting designs we were able to find. The beetles were used as a hand wash board and, since there must be much pressure during the washing process, they were made of the hardest wood.

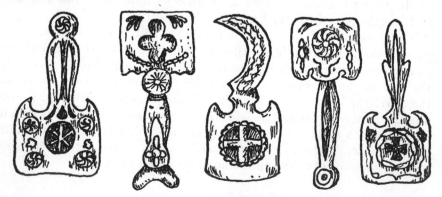

Figure 5. Washing Beetles.

Figure 6. Wooden Signs.

These signs are crudely made and decorated, yet they have the charm of the folk people. They were used on gates, houses, or in front of stores or market places. We suggest that campers make similar signs and nail them in front of their tent or unit. These particular signs are from:

A. Switzerland. Note that each fish has different markings.
B. Flanders. This design has also been reproduced in iron.
C. and D. Swedish signs cut from wood and used on gates.

Figure 7. Wooden Drinking Cups.

Figure 8. Carved Bird.

Whittling

A knife is one of the peasant's most treasured possessions and he uses it with skill and dexterity. Since most campers are versed in the art of whittling, we will not go into techniques except to stress the importance of selecting a soft wood and keeping the knife blade sharp at all times. Make a drawing of your project on a block of wood showing front, side and rear views as shown in Figure 8. Cut away a little wood at a time until you have a general outline and then begin adding features.

Figures 8 and 9 show typical nature projects whittled from wood.

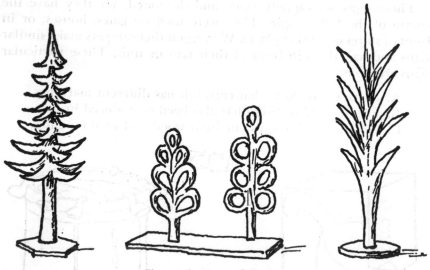

Figure 9. Carved Trees.

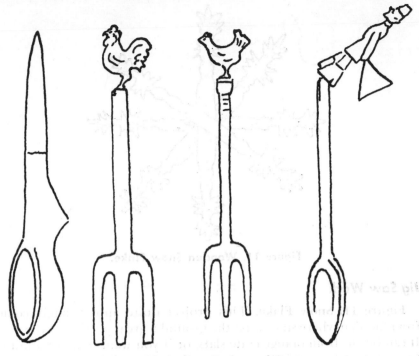

Figure 10. Italian Forks and Spoons.

Here are wooden spoons and forks made by Italian peasants. Choose a block of wood that has a fine grain and draw on an outline of the fork or spoon. Be sure the handle and prongs run lengthwise of the grain. If you want to carve a bird or figure on top of the handle, be sure to make it first, prongs next and finally the handle.

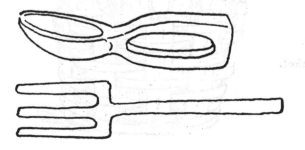

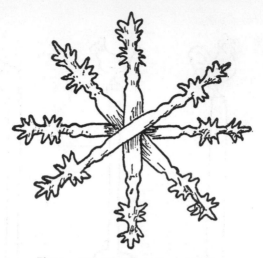

Figure 11. Wooden Snow Flake.

Jig Saw Work

Figure 11. Snow Flake. This project quite appropriately comes from Sweden where snow is on the ground a great portion of the year. It can be cut from orange crate slats, or if you want to make a miniature snow flake, cut it from tongue depressors. Tiny, wooden snow flakes make charming tree ornaments.

Figure 12. Basket Stays. This is another idea from Sweden. The basket stays or ribs are cut from ½" pine strips and a jig saw is used to cut out flowers or birds on the protruding end. If you want to use this type basket for fire wood, omit the handle.

Figure 12.

Wood Basket.

136

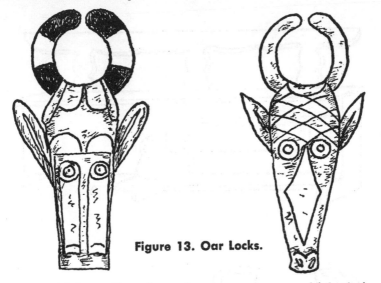

Figure 13. Oar Locks.

Since the Africans live along the waterways on which their very existence depends, many of their crafts have to do with decorating their boats. They build their crafts with great dexterity and skill. One of the simpler crafts is to decorate the oar locks.

**Figure 14.
Wooden Lanterns.**

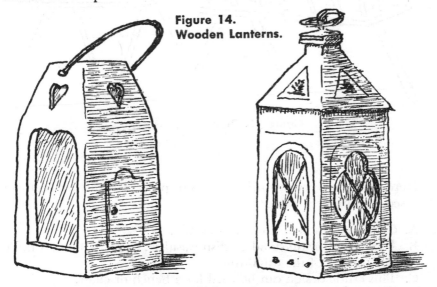

Wooden lanterns were used throughout Europe for many centuries. You may find dozens of designs by looking through old books in your public library. Here are two typical lanterns, A—made of wood and B—made of tin.

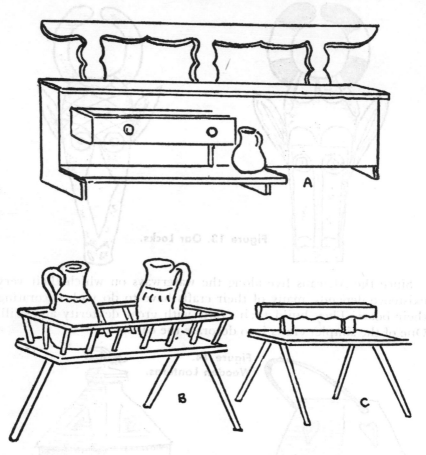

Figure 15. Pioneer Furniture.

Here are some very primitive pieces of peasant furniture that can be used in a pioneer camp:

A. Combination bench and wash stand.
B. A rack for a wash stand or dish washing. Note that it has three legs instead of the usual four.
C. This crude design can be used for a bench or chair.

Kites

Kites have been made and flown by people in every country in the world, but it is with China that we associate this ancient craft most closely. All China thinks, plans and builds kites for the Carnival of the Winds, which is also called "Feast of Ascending on High." Some of the kites flown on that day are really beautiful and some are grotesque and varied in shape. Huge aerial monsters are launched requiring a dozen men to launch and another crew to control the flying ropes. During the winter, the man who is worried makes his kite, writes all his woes on its tail, and on the day of the festival goes to a hill and literally flies his troubles away into the blue. The kites are most colorful and varied as to theme. Some are dragon flies a hundred times larger than the original; moths, beetles and birds of brilliant plumage are also represented. Then there are the frightening ones of dragons or bats and grotesque faces. Fish are the favorite themes because they bring good luck.

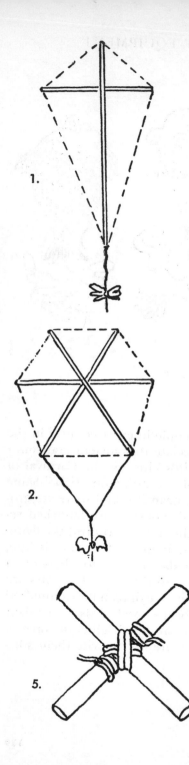

1.

2.

3.

4.

5.

6.

How to Make a Kite

In order to build a kite, there are a few principles that must be followed. You must first decide on the face and the size of your kite. There are four general shapes, Figures 1, 2, 3, and 4, so draw an outline of the motif you wish to use and decide which type frame it will require. Cut the face out of paper or cloth and stretch over the frame.

Strips of spruce board or bamboo are best for the framework. The board must be the right length—just the length of the kite to be built. For a kite three feet long, use wood that is three feet long and ¼ inch square. Split the board into proper lengths. For a four foot length kite, use a ⅜ inch stick and for a kite five feet long, use a ½ inch square stick.

Balance the sticks in the middle and lash them together. See illustrations on opposite page for square and diagonal lashing, Figures 5 and 6. Use glue to assist in the lashing. See that the cloth or paper cover does not buckle the frame.

After the sticks are lashed the paper or cloth is stretched over the frame and glued at the edges. Next you must make a *bridle* with stout string indicated by the dotted lines in the drawings. Place tail pieces about one foot apart. If made in several pieces, you may then make adjustments for varying wind conditions. The bridles for the other kites follow this principle and you can follow the dotted lines.

The ordinary method of constructing a tail is to fasten slips of paper six inches apart along a piece of string. The tail should be fifteen to twenty times the length of the kite. Wind the flying string on a stick, thus avoiding knots and kinks. It is well to have a friend hold the kite against the wind. The friend should stand at a distance of twenty-five yards from the person flying the kite. It is usually helpful to run a short distance when the wind lifts the kite. Play out the string slowly and when the kite is flying well the string may be let out faster. Be sure to select a large vacant lot or field from which to fly your kite. In the excitement of launching it, you will forget about the hazards under foot or in the air. However, never fly a kite near an electric power line!

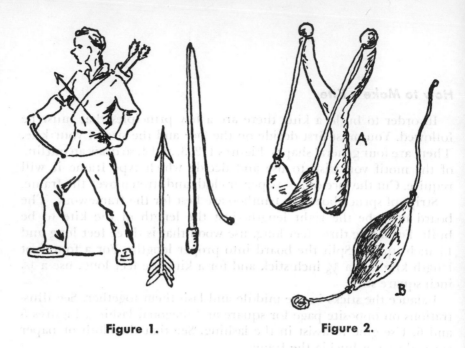

Figure 1.   **Figure 2.**

Whip Bow. In every country children have played with bows and arrows, but here is a simple whip bow (Figure 1) that can be made in a few minutes by any boy. The bow is made from an elastic sapling and bound at the top and bottom with string or leather thong. The whip lash is a stout string attached to the small end of the sapling and a strong knot tied at the other end. The arrow is cut of pine shingle with a notch cut at the blunt end for inserting the arrow before shooting. The spear point is sharpened as an ordinary arrow. The knot in the string prevents the arrow from slipping off the string until it is shot by the archer. The whip bow in the hands of the boy in the illustration shows how it is held before shooting.

Sling. These devices for hurling stones have been used since before Biblical times and were man's earliest weapons. The type of sling shown in Figure 2A is used today by children to shoot paper wads, peas or pebbles. It is a piece of leather attached to a forked stick by two pieces of elastic. Figure 2B shows an older type of sling cut out of an oval piece of leather about two inches wide at the broadest part. At each end is fastened a leather thong or piece of cord, one being longer than the other. A stone is placed in the broadest part of the leather and the longest cord twisted twice or three times around the hand. Whirl it around several times and let go the shorter cord.

142

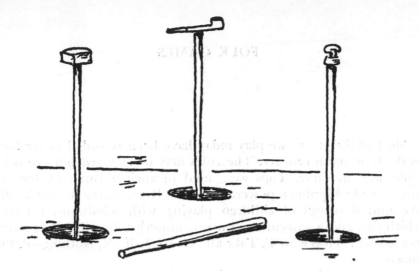

Knock Them Down

A number of holes, usually three, are dug about six inches in diameter and set in the form of a triangle. In each is placed a pole about five feet high and on the top is set some small article of no great value, such as a pipe or tobacco box, etc. The game consists of knocking off these articles with a stick. It is no use to strike a pole that supports an article. The pole will only fall away and let the article itself fall into the hole. This hit does not count and the stick has to be replaced. The only possible way of knocking the articles off so as to fall clear of the holes is to strike them full and fair with the throwing stick which is by no means easy.

Novette

A bridge is made of slats of wood about two and a half or three inches wide. Fasten them together as shown in the illustration. The players use circular discs of wood the diameter of which measures about an inch less than the arches. The discs are sometimes painted in different colors and sometimes all painted alike. The usual mode of playing the game is for each player in turn to take a disc and try to bowl from a stated distance from the numbered arches. When he has delivered all his discs, the numbers are added together and the one who has the greatest number scores.

Most of the games we play today have been recorded as far back as the fourteenth century. The rules may be changed but the principles are the same. Tops were used in ancient times by boys in Greece and whipping tops were known in Rome in the days of Virgil. We find drawings of children playing with windmills, marbles, whirligigs, and a fifteenth century manuscript describes a te-totum as a four-sided top with T, Take all—H, For half—N, Nothing—P, Put Down.

Since the making of game equipment is an important folk craft, we will describe a few that are traditional in different countries.

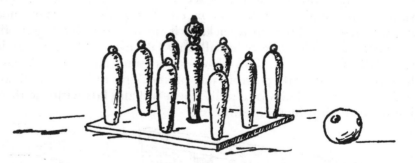

Dutch Pins

Nine wooden pins are set upright on a frame, the central pin being called the king and having a crown on its head. A very large and heavy ball is thrown from a short distance, and the thrower counts one for each pin and two for the king.

An old game called "Devil among Tailors" is a variation of this game. Nine small pins are placed in the midst of a circular board surrounded by a ledge. Players spin peg tops alternately and he who beats down the pins to the number of one-and-thirty wins.

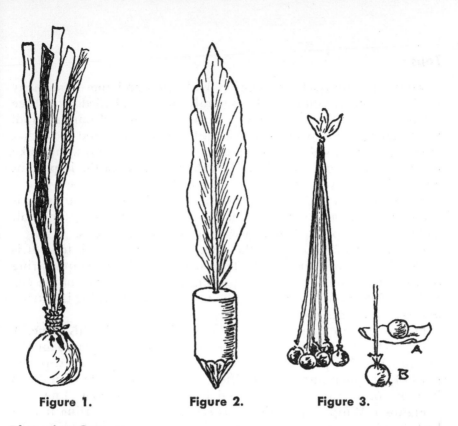

| Figure 1. | Figure 2. | Figure 3. |

Throwing Games

Figure 1. The Comet. Long colored streamers are attached to a ball or rock encased in a leather cover. They are used particularly at carnivals and public gatherings.

Figure 2. Darts. Darts is a favorite game in almost every country. The darts are made by shaping a piece of light wood and inserting a needle at the point. Feathers are used to balance the dart.

Figure 3. Bolas. This is a sling used for hunting in Africa and Australia. The principle can be applied to a game for the out of doors. Select six round stones of equal size and wrap each stone in a piece of old cloth or leather as shown in Figure 3A. Take three pieces of string, each five feet long, and double them in the center and bind the double parts together; a few small feathers may be added to the top or colored streamers. To the ends of the strings attach the stones. To cast it—grasp the bolas by the feathered top with the thumb and forefinger, whirl it around your head and let it go. For target practice, use a number of reeds or sticks stuck upright in the ground about a foot apart and see how many reeds can be leveled on a single cast of the bolas.

Tops

Tops have always been favorites with boys and there are many kinds in as many countries. In general, tops are divided into three kinds, those that are being spun by means of throwing from the hand, those that are spun by means of a handle and a string, and those that are spun by means of a whip. To describe all of the tops would take too much space, so we are giving you the principles of the important ones and telling you about some others.

Figure 1. This is the oldest and most primitive of the tops. It is simple to make and is spun by hand. It can be amusing for small children if it is painted in narrow rings of various colors.

Figure 2. **Peg Top.** This is the queen of the game with tops. It is made of wood and can be gaily decorated. To spin it—wrap a string or whip cord around the top, beginning at the upper half of the peg and winding gradually upward. The top is spun by jerking the string as it is thrown into the ring.

Figure 3. **Chip Stone.** A wooden spoon is needed in this game. A large circle is made and some smooth flat stones are placed in the middle. The first player spins his top in the usual manner, slips the bowl of the spoon under it and lifts it off the ground. He then drops it on one of the stones and tries to drive it to the boundary line.

Figure 4. **Whip Top.** This top is easily set up by twirling it with both hands on a smooth surface, and applying a whip with gentleness at first, increasing the vigor of the blows, as the top gets firm on its peg. The whip is made of a long wooden handle to which are lashed long leather thongs. However, eel-skin was much preferred to cord or leather if it could be obtained.

Figure 5. **Humming Tops.** These are commercial tops made of light metal and hollow inside and make a humming sound as they spin. The Japanese were masters at making these tops. When the top is to be spun, the peg is held in the left hand while the string is drawn sharply with the right. This is the astonishing Japanese top that runs over bridges, climbs stairs, opens doors for itself and will even ring a door bell!

Figure 6. **French Top.** It consists of a case in which are a number of shallow, hollow, conical tops. Motion is given to them all by the same pull of the string, and a skillful player can keep them going for an astonishing time.

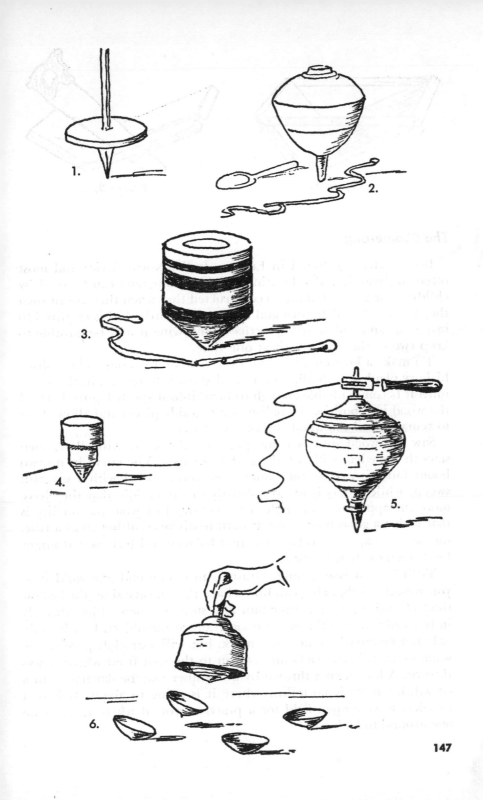

1. 2. 3. 4. 5. 6.

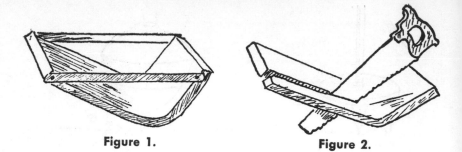

Figure 1.   Figure 2.

The Boomerang

Boomerangs are found in Europe, India, North Africa and most often in Australia. The hunting or play boomerang can be used by children for games and are so constructed that when they are thrown they make a complete turn and return. Very little skill is required to make one and with a little practice in throwing it may be possible to keep two or three in the air at one time.

To make a boomerang, scald a piece of well seasoned elm, ash or hickory plank with boiling water and allow it to remain in the water until it becomes pliable enough to bend into shape as Figure 1. Hold the wood into position by nailing on two side pieces and allow them to remain until the wood is thoroughly dry.

Saw the wood into as many pieces as the wood will allow, then smooth the edges with a knife and sandpaper. The curve in no two boomerangs is exactly the same; some come round with a graceful sweep; while others bend so suddenly in the middle that they have more the appearance of angles than curves. Just what the quality is that makes a good boomerang is hard to discover, although as a rule, the one that appears to have the best balance and feels as if it might be thrown easily is the best.

To Throw a Boomerang. Grasp it near one end and hold it as you would a club, being careful to have the concave side (the hollow side) turned from you. Take aim at a stone or some object directly in front of you, and throw the boomerang at the object. It will probably not go anywhere near the mark, but will soar aloft performing some extraordinary tricks and return to the spot from where it was thrown. A boomerang thrown by a beginner may be dangerous in a crowd, for there is no telling where it is going to alight. It is best to select a wide open field for a practice ground where there is no one around to be hurt.

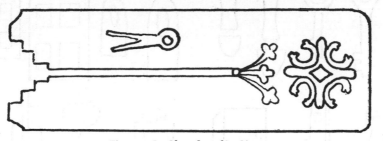

Figure 1. Shepherd's Sign.

The crafts of the shepherds are pure examples of folk art—they are entirely functional and express a spiritual quality that can only be acquired by those living alone and under the stars. The shepherd spends long winter hours in his cottage but, even so, his craft has to do with his preparation for the spring journey and care of his flock. We can only describe a few of his projects but we hope they will stimulate campers to go to the library and do some research on their own.

The Hook and Crook. The shepherd's most important piece of equipment is his staff at the top of which is a hook and crook. We can understand the old saying "We will get it by hook or crook" when we know how the shepherd handles his staff. The end of the staff is usually made of iron and the crook at the top is used for hooking a sheep by the leg and drawing it in from the flock. The hook is used for holding an object while the staff is carried over the shoulder. The British shepherds carry small kegs of water, while some keep a small bag of pebbles or bits of turf tied to the end. They use these to throw at the sheep.

Figure 2. The Hook and Crook.

149

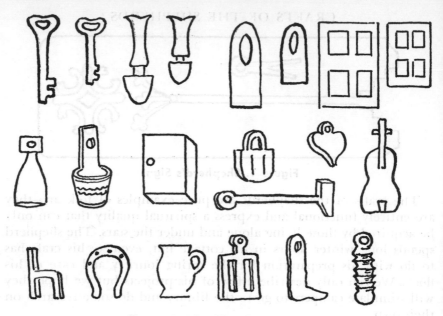

Figure 3. Identification Markers.

Extremely interesting are the methods which are still customary in many parts of Europe of distinguishing the young lamb and mother sheep. The shepherd takes a couple of small pieces of wood and carves out a familiar object such as a horseshoe, key, hammer, pot, etc. One is larger than the other, the smaller one being destined for the lamb.

Shepherd's charms are little wooden objects carved out of wood and worn during the summer as they tend their flocks. The shape has significance only to the wearer who chooses an object that appeals to him.

Figure 4. Shepherd's Charms.

Figure 5. Hungarian Shepherd's Purse.

Shepherd's Purse

A shepherd's purse is a very important part of his equipment. In it he keeps his small tools, toilet articles, food for the day, or any other small items he may need. As shown above, other small articles are tied to the outside of the bag such as his charm, match holder and a small utility bag.

To make a bag similar to the ones illustrated here, you will need a good piece of cowhide, at least for the flap in front, and a cheaper quality leather for side and back. From heavy paper cut a pattern the size and shape of the bag you wish to make and follow instructions for tooling leather.

The two bags illustrated below were chosen because of the interesting design of the large one and the function of the small one. The pouch-like bag is used for carrying pebbles and bits of turf to throw at the sheep to make them travel in certain directions.

Figure 6. Shepherd's Purse and Bag.

Figure 7. Designs for Shepherd's Purses.

The three designs illustrated above are beautiful examples of folk art. The shoulder strap is cut into several pieces joined together with metal rings. The rings are used for attaching small objects that the shepherd wants to take on a journey.

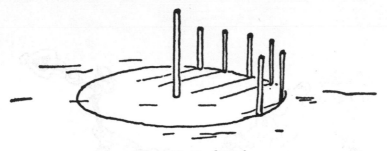

Figure 8. Turf Dial.

The shepherds had many ways of telling the time of day by the sun and stars but here is a simple dial that works very well. Select a small bit of ground and make a rough circle about 18″ in diameter with a pointed stick and leave the stick perpendicular in the ground at center of the circle. The south direction is ascertained by means of a compass. Having done this, fix another stick due west which is, of course, merely a matter of measurement. Now fix five sticks for the hours one to five inclusive, so completing a sun dial with seven gnomons on its circumference. At three o'clock on an October afternoon (which is about the time shown in the drawing), it may be time to return to the fold and the shadow of the third stick from the mid day gnomon will then fall on the central stick and the shepherd will know it is time to start.

Figure 9. Triangle Dial.

This dial is more similar to an ordinary dial. The central stick is the gnomon and a stick notched for the hours is laid across the ends of the two other sticks, pointing due north and due east.

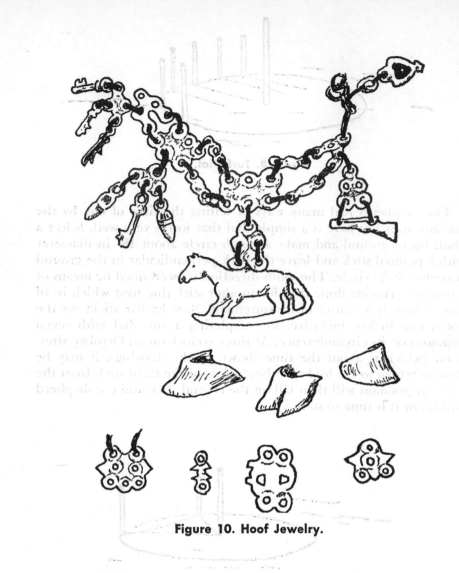

Figure 10. Hoof Jewelry.

This novel jewelry is carved from pieces of animal hoofs and polished to a high degree. Note the chain part and pendants are medallion-like pieces with small holes so they can be fastened together with metal links. To these parts are attached charms and tokens designed by the shepherds.

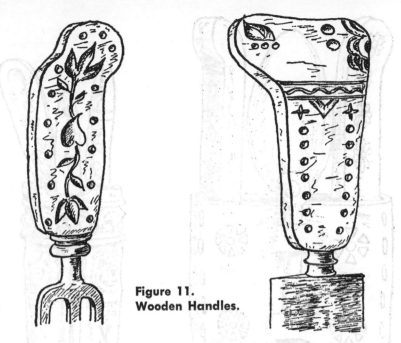

**Figure 11.
Wooden Handles.**

These handles are cut from hard wood and carved decorations added according to the contour of the stick. Sometimes the designs are burned on but more often they are carved out with a knife. The beauty of the shepherd's utensils is the high polish they receive by rubbing them over and over again with the sheep wool. The oil acts not only as a wood filler, but brings out gleaming highlights by rubbing with the palm of the hand.

The making of a match box was a necessary craft as the matches were in constant use and had to be kept dry. There are a number of match boxes and holders in the Leather chapter, but we are adding this one from Hungary because of its interesting design.

Figure 12. Match Box.

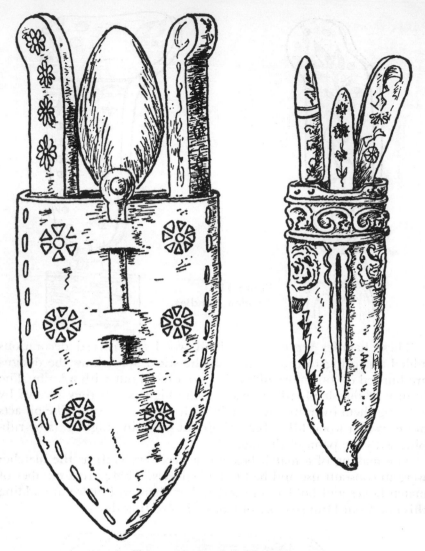

Figure 13. Leather Sheaths.

Here are two interesting sheaths designed for carrying a knife, fork and spoon. The usual loop for fitting around a belt is missing as the shepherd carried it in his purse. However, two loops can be added just back of the knife and fork. Make the sheath from cowhide and sew together with a saddle stitch.

Poker Work

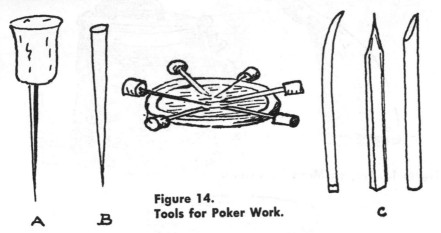

A   B

Figure 14.
Tools for Poker Work.

C

Poker work is a decoration on wood produced by burning on the design with a red hot instrument. In this country we call it wood burning but originally a hot poker was used—hence the name. The shepherds practiced this primitive way of decorating their tools and utensils while they were outdoors. It is almost impossible to get an evenness of line so the design must be free with bold strokes and little detail. The whole effect is one of rugged picturesqueness and well associated with the life of the shepherd.

The greatest drawback in using a poker for burning in a design is that the point cools as soon as it is applied to the wood and must be constantly reheated. As an alternative, large steel needles or nails shaped as shown above are used. It is best to have a number heating at one time around a burner as illustrated above. The design can be treated in two ways—one, the background burned away so the design stands up in relief, or the design can be burned down into the background. In either case, you will need a number of sharp instruments shaped as in Figure 14C so they can fit into curves, flatten a background or burn a fine line. It is very easy to shape the points of nails by filing them to a desired shape and the drawing suggests three useful forms. Whether you use steel needles or nails, you must protect your hands by adding a wooden handle at one end as shown in Figure 14A.

Any wood may be used for this type of decoration, but the design will be more prominent if the background is light in color such as pine or maple. Smooth the wood and trace on the design with a pencil indicating the part to be burned by shading. Add a coat of shellac, rub with fine steel wool and wax.

Figure 15. Projects Made from Horn.

Horn Craft

This craft has been developed to the highest degree by the shepherds. For many centuries designs were applied to the horns by using hand-made chisels and it was a long, tedious process. Today, the designs are painted on the horn with asphaltum and allowed to dry. The horn is then placed in a bath of ⅔ water and ⅓ nitric acid until the acid eats away the background. For complete instructions, turn to Etching on Metal. You may add color to the design by using oils. Here are some suggested projects:

    A. Bottle—a wooden bottom and cork is added.

    B. This box was really used by the shepherds to hold lotion for the sheep. It has a hinged lid and handle on top so it can be tied to the belt or purse.

    C. Box with a carved wooden lid.

    D. Drinking cup that can be carried over the shoulder without spilling the water.

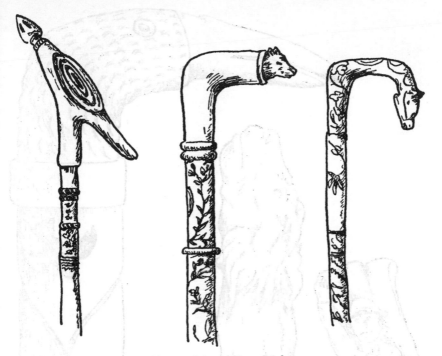

Figure 16. Alpine Sticks.

Hiking Sticks

These hiking sticks are made in varied designs according to the original shape of the wood or purpose for which it is to be used. If you want to make one of your own, it should be planned very carefully because it can be personalized and become a memento of many hikes and camping trips. First of all, you should find just the right limb or branch that has an interesting twist at the top so it can be carved as shown in the illustration. Keep an open mind as you go along and let your imagination work if you find an interesting shape and decide how it can be modeled into an object by adding a few features.

First of all, remove the bark and shape the stick so it is the correct length and tapers toward the bottom. Carve the staff and add decoration by removing background so design will stand up in relief. This can be done with small chisels or a sharp knife. Note that the decoration on one stick on the following page tells a story of travelers along a mountain trail. Shepherds often recorded a summer log, or kept a record of lambs born by adding notches in the stick.

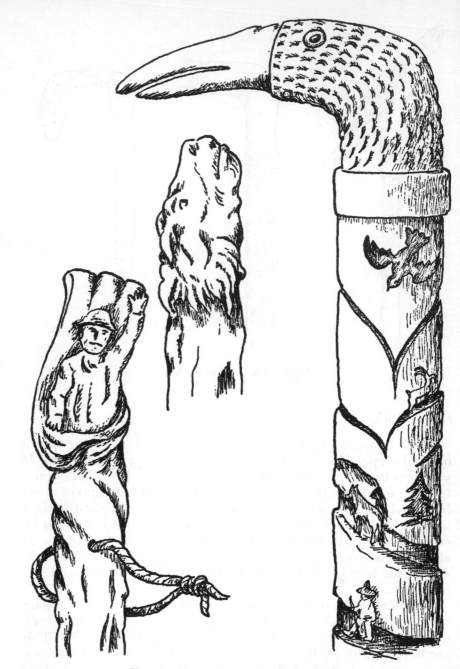

Figure 17. Decorated Walking Sticks.

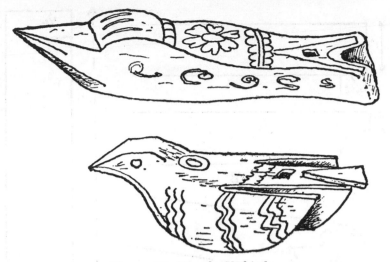

Figure 18. Wooden Whistles.

The principle upon which a whistle is made is to have a small opening at the top of the piece that fits into the mouth so that air is blown into the small chamber about ½" from the lips. The back wall becomes a sounding board that sends out sound waves through a small opening at the top. Figure 19A shows a detailed drawing of the sound chamber in the tail of the birds. The shepherds developed whistles that can be heard a mile away by their dogs yet cannot be heard by a person standing nearby.

Figure 19B shows how a willow whistle can be made. Use a green willow twig and loosen the bark by tapping on all sides with a knife. Slip out the wood and shape the end as shown in the illustration. Cut a window in the bark and slip the wood back into place. Slant the end to form a mouthpiece.

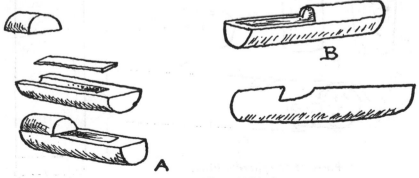

Figure 19. Willow Whistles.

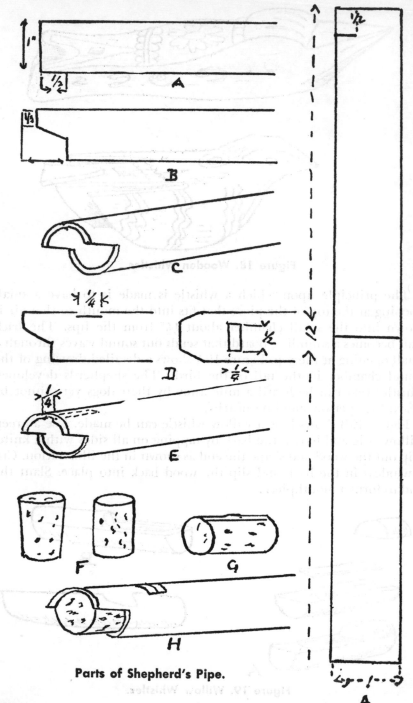

Parts of Shepherd's Pipe.

How to Make a Shepherd's Pipe

You can make a shepherd's pipe for yourself by following the directions given below and, what is more, you can learn to play it even though you have never had a music lesson. The shepherds played it at night and that is the time it gives forth its sweetest tones.

You will need a piece of bamboo 12″ long and one inch thick. Bamboo cut into proper lengths can be purchased at handicraft and scouting supply houses. You will also need a cork to fit tightly into the end of the bamboo tube. For tools, a pen-knife or other good knife, and a small saw—preferably a coping saw—are required. A set of files will make the job easier: one long round file, and three flat ones—flat, round and three-cornered. To make the pipe, you must take the following steps:

A. First make the inside of the bamboo wall clean by using the long file.

B. Select the end farther away from the joint, measure one-half inch from this end and saw half way through.

C. Work from the same end, mark about one-third inch down and cut slantwise to meet the end of the first cut so as to shape it for a mouthpiece.

D. Cut a window on the top side, one inch from the end of the mouthpiece. The window should measure one-half inch across the tube and one-quarter inch lengthwise of the tube. Clean the edge of the window with your file and make the side away from the mouthpiece slantwise.

E. File an air passage from the mouthpiece to the window, using the flat side of your three-cornered file.

F. File your cork into a perfect cylinder just the right size to fit snugly into the tube. Cut away a little at a time with a sharp razor blade if necessary.

G. Flatten one side of the cork to match the air passage in the mouthpiece and shove it in until it reaches the edge of the window as shown below.

H. Cut off the end of the cork and cut it slantwise to match the mouthpiece you have cut in the tube.

You are now ready to tune your pipe.

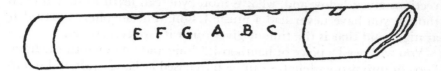

How to Tune a Shepherd's Pipe

Blow gently into the pipe through the wind passage. The tone you get is the lowest note possible according to the length and the bore. You can, if you wish, use whatever pitch you happen to get, but for convenience in tuning and uniformity if you have several Shepherd's Pipes, we suggest that you tune to D (the next white note after middle C).

Sound your low tone. It will probably be a little lower than middle D, and the way to raise it is to cut off the end of the pipe until it is high enough. Cut off not more than one-quarter of an inch at a time. You can raise the pitch by shortening the pipe but you cannot lower it.

When you get your D tone, measure off one-quarter of the length of the whole pipe and mark the first hole, starting from the end away from the mouthpiece. Make a small hole and sound it. It should sound the next note of the scale (E on the piano). If it sounds flat, use the file to bring it a little nearer to the mouthpiece. If it is sharp, use a little plastic wood to move the hole farther away from the mouthpiece. Be sure this tone is the right pitch before continuing.

Now add another hole about seven-eights of an inch nearer the mouthpiece. Tune as before to the third note in the scale.

Lessen the distance between holes, and continue until you have six holes, the last two three-quarters of an inch apart. Tune each hole before making the next. Your ear will tell you how it should sound, but compare it with a piano if there is one at hand. You can also use a pitch pipe for tuning.

Now make the last hole on the underneath side, directly under the hole nearest your window. This will sound D an octave higher than your first tone and gives you the complete shepherd's pipe.

164

Playing the Shepherd's Pipe

Hold the pipe in both hands as illustrated above and number each note according to the number of holes covered. For example, when only the left thumb is down, we will call the note "1." When all seven holes are covered, you may call the note "7." Follow this system of numbering and play the following familiar tunes. If you can read music, you may find it easier to play by note instead of number.

165

OH, SUSANNA

7-6   5   3   3 2 3 5   7 6 5 5   6   7   6
I   come from   A- la- ba- ma   with a ban- jo   on   my knee,

7-6   5   3   3 2 3 5   7   6 5 5   6 6   7
I'm   goin' to   Lou-si-a-na   my   Su- san- na   for to   see;

7-6   5   3   3   2 3 5 7   6   7 5   6 7   6
It   rained all night the day I left, the wea-ther it was dry,

7-6   5 3 3   2 3 5   7   6 5 5   6 6   7
The   sun so hot   I froze to death,   Su-san- na, don't you cry.

  4   4   2   2   2   3   3 5 7   6
Oh, Su- san- na,   Oh, don't you cry for me,

  7   6 5   3   3 2 3 5   7 6 5 5   6 6   7
For   I come from   A- la-ba- ma   with my ban- jo   on my knee.

FOR HE'S A JOLLY GOOD FELLOW

7-6   5 5 5   6   5   4 5   5   8   6 6 7   6
For he's a jol- ly good fel-low,   for he's a jol- ly good

              5   7
             fel- low,

6   5 5 5 6 5   4 2   2   3 3 3 4   6   7
For he's a jol-ly good fel- low,   which no-bo- dy can de- ny.

          5   3 3   3   2   2   3
      Which   no- bo- dy   can de- ny,
      Which   no- bo- dy   can de- ny,

7-6   5 5 5   6   5   4 6   5   6   6 6 7   6
For he's a jol- ly good fel-low,   for he's a jol- ly good

             5   7
            fel- low,

6   5 5 5 6 5   4 2   2   3 3 3 4   6   7
For he's a jol- ly good fel- low,   which. no-bo- dy can de- ny.

5. Crafts for Entertainment

MANY FOLK CRAFTS were applied to devices for entertaining and amusing the public. Since the population was more or less rural, the shows were planned for small groups. They were usually brought before the public by roving showmen who charged a small fee for a few minutes of entertainment. Among these devices that required a great deal of originality and skill on the part of the craftsman were peep shows, panoramas, puppets, marionettes and mechanical toys. The principles involved in these shows were used in almost every country and are still used today. We have selected several interesting types of puppets and peep shows to describe as they are practical for use in camps or churches for entertaining small groups.

Figure 1. Mechanical Puppet.

This is one of the oldest types of puppets on record, dating from the fourteenth century. They consist of jointed wooden figures through the center of which a string is passed, to be held by a player at each end. They are made of wood, dressed in armor and the legs are weighted to give balance to the body. The strings are jerked back and forth and with the tightening and slackening of the cord, the body moves.

Figure 2. Punch and Judy Stage.

Punch and Judy

Punch and Judy are two grotesque figures with hooked noses that have brought fun and merriment to people for several centuries. Their drama dealt with situations in every-day life, enlivened with slapstick and buffoonery. The oldest show of this type was probably seen in Italy where the principal character was Pulcinello, a shy comic servant who was continually getting in and out of scrapes and cleverly escaping punishment. This comedy was eventually introduced in France where Pulcinello became Polichinelle, a witty, Gallic character still to be seen and loved by rural people.

England not only rechristened Polichinelle as Punch but also gave him Judy for a wife. During the years, other characters were added to help dramatize the stories but Punch was always a quarrelsome nuisance to the others, particularly Judy. The whole dialogue was in satire with Judy the nagging wife, the baby being thrown out the window, blows being stopped by the policeman and continual screams in a high, squeaky voice. At the close of the play, the devil would come to carry Punch away and even the hangman was called upon wherever the crime warranted the extreme penalty.

There are many types and sizes of stages that can be used for a Punch and Judy show. Since the puppets rest on the hands, there must be openings in the bottom of the stage through which the hand and wrist can be thrust. The frame of the stage is made of cardboard or plywood while the cross pieces of wood at the bottom are just large enough to hold the stage together. The stage should be set at the shoulder height of the puppeteers so they can stand while manipulating the puppets.

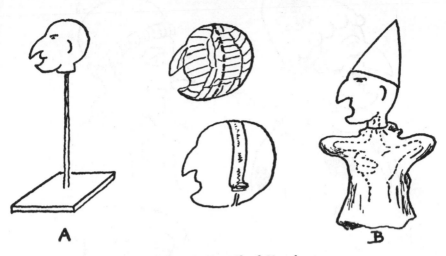

Figure 3. Detail of Head.

To make a papier mâché head, first make a model of the head from plasteline and place it on a stick which is fastened to a wooden base as shown in Figure 3A. Cut away excess plasteline with modeling tools.

Now cover the head with several layers of small pieces of paper which have been dipped into flour paste. It is a good idea to use a different color paper for each layer as the small pieces should be placed evenly over the surface. Allow the paper to dry thoroughly and then remove from the model by cutting it in a line around the top of the head and down each side so the head can be taken away in two pieces. Seal the two parts together by using strips of paper covered with paste as shown in Figure 3. Also, seal in a hollow cardboard tube about five inches long at the neck to be used for inserting the fore-finger to manipulate the head.

Next, cover the entire surface of the head with a layer of fine paper after the ridges have been removed with sandpaper. Paper toweling makes a good cover as the texture is right for receiving paint for the features. Make a simple dress with two tiny arms into which the thumb and middle fingers are used for arms. Make the costumes as suggested in the drawings in Figure 4.

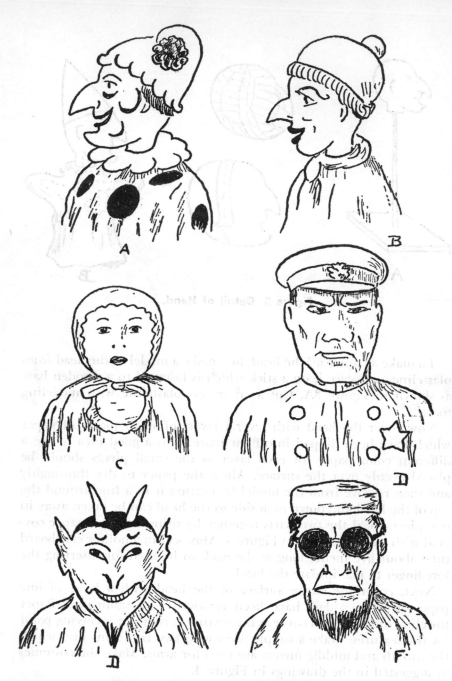

Figure 4. Punch and Judy Characters.

A—Punch, B—Judy, C—Baby, D—Policeman, E—Devil, F—Hangman.

Peep Shows

Peep shows were many and varied both as to shape and subject. Just the fact that the scene was enclosed in a box with a single hole through which one peeked was in itself intriguing. In England, the traveling showman had little houses or stages which he carried about on his back and then set up on a platform for viewing as shown in the above drawing. Peep shows were also popular in the pubs or taverns where the themes were not always in the best of taste. In the cities, the peep shows were found on busy street corners and were always found at carnivals and county fairs.

The principle upon which a peep show is built is to enclose a space into which two or three dimensional figures are placed in some kind of setting. The box is illuminated by covering the top and sometimes the bottom with transparent paper through which rays can penetrate. One type of show was a single lithograph at the back which was a picture of the center hall of Prince Albert's Museum. In ordinary light, you would see the great hall with light shining through tiny holes to simulate lighted candles in the chandeliers. When light would be turned on at the back the picture would entirely change and the tiny lights come from the Tower of London.

The making of a peep show is an excellent craft for school or camp since it involves carpentry, painting and lighting. The figures and parts of the setting, such as trees and small houses, can be most effective when made of clay and glazed in color. The bisque foundations can be easily cemented on to the bottom of the box.

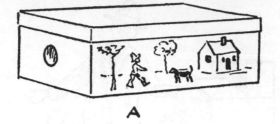

A

B

B

C

Figure 5. Types of Peep Shows.

Figure 5A. This shows the simplest type of peep show that can be made in an ordinary shoe box. Paint the interior in a color to fit the setting and then, if it is a room, make period furniture. For exterior scenes, small trees and houses are necessary. Since you can see only the fronts of the figures while peeping through the hole, you need decorate only one side as you set them in place. Motifs cut from greeting cards can be used very well by young children who wish to make their own show. After the scene is complete, cut a small hole at the front of the box and cover the top with a piece of transparent paper.

Figure 5B. This is a more elaborate show and is lighted both from the top and bottom. It is made by cutting any number of squares of cardboard (depending on what size peep show you wish to make) and drawing a scene on each card. Cut away the background with a sharp knife so the characters and trees stand in silhouette with a vacant place in the middle so you can view the entire length of the box. Paint them in appropriate colors. This type of show can be collapsed by folding the top and bottom papers into accordion pleats as shown in the illustration. Make a flat box or envelope a little larger than the squares for storing away the show.

Figure 5C. Many of the Easter eggs had winter scenes, using piles of sugar to resemble snow. The tiny figures were carried into the egg by fastening them on a long, slender stick in such a manner that they could be stood in place and the stick removed.

The German Dwarf

This parlor game requires two people to manipulate the dwarf, a table with a long cloth and a pair of curtains. The body is made ahead of time and should be as large as a good size rag doll. In Germany, the dress is always very extravagant, as shown in the illustration and in bright, gay colors. However, the figure can be made to fit a certain theme if it is planned according to season or for different age groups.

The taller of the two persons chosen to enact the part of the dwarf disguises his face with a false mustache, wig, hat, etc. He pulls a pair of stockings over his hands and inserts them in a pair of shoes ornamented with bright buckles. The shorter of the two, standing behind, thrusts his arms as far as they will go under the other's armpits and into sleeves of the bodice. The fun of the entertainment is to listen to the dwarf's patter and see how he coordinates his hands and feet to suit the lines. For an informal party, an extemporaneous dialogue is best because half the fun is watching to see if the gestures express what the voice is saying. A rehearsed skit can be perfectly coordinated and will draw great applause, particularly if it is a song or dance.

174

Figure 6. Toy Theatre.

This theatre is made from a large box with one side removed for the front of the stage. Small slits are cut in the bottom for inserting trees or other scenery as a setting for the play. It is necessary to cut holes at both ends for inserting the characters as the play proceeds. The figures are made of cardboard and features added with paint or crayon. If you wish to be less creative cut the figures and scenery from magazines and strengthen them by mounting on cardboard. To manipulate the figures, fit them into a tiny trough made of tin to which a long wire is fastened at one end as shown in Figure 7. The characters can be moved back and forth across the stage as the story is being told.

Figure 7. Detail of Manipulating Rods.

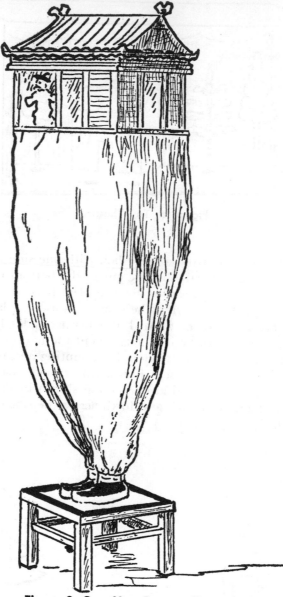

Figure 8. One Man Puppet Show.

These ingenious puppeteers wandered about China in the time of Marco Polo. The curtain was pulled up over the body of the showman and the stage rested on the top of the head. All extra puppets and stage equipment were kept in pockets at the waist where they could be easily changed while the show was in progress.

Figure 9. Puppet Screen.

Shadow Puppets

There are two types of shadow puppets—one, where the figures are cut in silhouettes from opaque material such as cardboard and only the outline shows on the screen. The others are very ornate figures, dressed in gold and silk kimonos with ornaments in colors to represent precious stones. Both types require a transparent screen on which can be painted scenery according to the theme of the play. The silhouette type of puppet is played behind the screen and the ornate ones in front. A screen such as the one shown in Figure 9 is suitable and can be made in any size to suit the puppets. Make the scenery from colored crepe paper and sew in place on a muslin screen. The arms and legs of the puppets are jointed and to each extremity is fastened a wire or stick which is moved to animate the body.

African Shadow Puppets.

In Africa, shadow puppets are made and operated by different tribes. They were most often associated with religion and superstitions and were used by witches and medicine men. In many parts of the country tribe idols have been found with secret controls which cause them to move and mystify the people. The figures were most often grotesque as they were used to frighten rather than entertain the people.

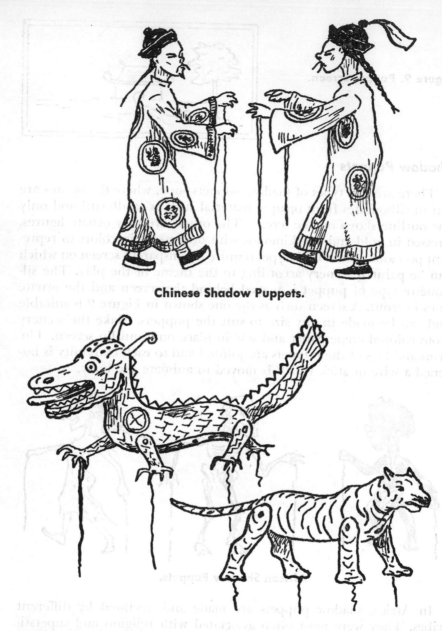

Chinese Shadow Puppets.

The Chinese animated their dragons and animals as well as people. They were made of transparent parchment and many parts were cut away and colored silk added to give life to the figure. The puppets were often made life-size so that the screen would extend across the entire theatre.

178

Figure 10. Chinese Cloth Puppets.

These puppets dressed in fine silk and embroidered in colors are extremely beautiful. They are often found in Chinese stores in this country, but very few people recognize them as puppets. The figures vary in size according to the stage on which they are shown. First cut a silhouette of the figure from cardboard and cover the front with a thin layer of cotton. The cotton is held in place by paste. The head is then covered with flesh colored silk and hair and features added with embroidery stitches. Dress the body in a silk kimono and applique on two hands, using the flesh colored silk. The figures are only three-fourths natural height, so make them in a sitting position.

The stage is made as shown in Figure 11. The opening should be at arm's height of puppeteers so they can stand while manipulating the figures. Note the curtain extends far enough on either side of the stage opening to cover the persons giving the show. There is a metal groove at the bottom of the stage along which the puppets are pushed while the story is read and action taking place. You will need several extra troughs in which to set up the characters as scenery and all are passed along in pantomime as the story unfolds. For instance, if a person is sitting under a tree he remains there all the time he is pushed across the screen.

These puppets are not animated in any way but are simply pushed across the stage in tempo with the story teller. If one of the characters must suddenly disappear, take it off with a notched stick such as the one shown in Figure 12.

Figure 11. Puppet Stage.

If you don't want an elaborate stage such as the one shown above, use a screen containing three panels. Cut an opening in the center panel for the stage and the other two panels will serve to hide the puppeteers. Decorate the screen in Chinese motifs.

Figure 12. Detail of Track and Rod.

FESTIVALS

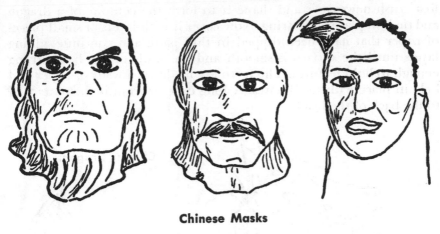

Chinese Masks

Chinese New Year

If you don't know about the Chinese New Year, you should seek information in your public library because it is one of the great world celebrations. Unlike our New Year, it begins the first day of the first moon which means any time between January 21st and February 19th. It was known as the Festival of Yüan Tan and was celebrated for fourteen days in all the cities in China. On each of the fourteen days, a special theme was carried out, such as the first day was Family Day. All members of the family and their household gathered together and feasted on a meatless diet. Another feature was that they wore their best clothes and, if they could afford it, bought all new garments from skin out. On the fifth day all houses were cleaned from top to bottom and the dust scattered on running water if there was a stream near by. On one of the days was the Feast of the Lanterns when all of China was aglow with tens of thousands of gaily decorated paper lanterns. In this country, we are more familiar with the dragon that goes up and down the streets demanding that the people give him alms or be destroyed. He has a large papier mâché head to which is fastened a long red velvet train beautifully embroidered with gold thread. A dozen or more men form the legs of the dragon by getting under the cape and the two men in front hold the head high with their arms and hands. In front are a number of masked men playing Chinese gongs and drums. While they lead the dragon along the street, the men dance to the peculiar rhythms thus making the body go up and down in a grotesque manner.

The head of the dragon is made from papier mâché and painted in bright green and gold. In order to make the head, you should first crush newspaper and shape it to form the contour of a dragon and tie it in place with string. Now cover it with layers of small pieces of paper that have been dipped in thin paste and continue adding layers until the surface is smooth and the walls of the head strong enough to hold features. The teeth are made with wads of paper and held in place with small wires. A long cape or train is then attached to the back of the head.

Chinese Dragon.

A dragon, such as the one illustrated above, can be seen in our own Chinatowns at the New Year. It goes up and down the streets and masked men play the drums with great noise and clatter as it stops in front of each house and tries to enter! To keep it from coming in, long strings of edibles with dollar bills tied intermittently are hung from the windows to feed the dragon. They are released and put into a cart which is pulled along in the rear. Coins are thrown into the cape by spectators as the dragon goes along the street.

182

Carnival at Nice

One of the great celebrations in Europe is the carnival at Nice where all day and far into the night grotesque, caricatured figures of fact and fiction possess the city. The weird creatures with deformed, nodding heads parade down Avenue de la Gare and the streets are alive with many colored lights and large, gorgeous butterflies are caught in golden webs hung across the avenue. The king of the carnival dresses in striped hose, a slashed doublet, and, grasping in his right hand a sceptre in the image of a jester with cap and bells, leads the parade in a float draped in purple velvet.

Many of the floats are subtle, piercing sarcasm that only the French can manufacture and the people in the streets shake with laughter as they pass by. Many favorite characters are taken out of storage year after year, such as gigantic cabbages and carrots and gnomes and elphin people that lead the parade. Next come devils mounted on horseback followed by eight horses dragging a papier mâché lion twenty feet high and length in proportion to the head. On top stands Tartain of Turocon to tame the wild beast. Behind can be seen the Washwoman of Var followed by every wonder of fairy extravagance as the nymphs and fairies appear, supplementing the grotesque.

As the fun becomes more excited, the spectators fill the streets and bombard everyone with confetti and plaster pellets. Around their necks are worn garlands of flowers and even the donkeys and carts brought in from the market places receive their share of the decorations.

Papier Mâché Masks

The pellets which the spectators throw are little round balls made from colored clay or plaster. Each person carries them in a little bag and often they are mixed with flower petals as they are thrown at the passers by. To protect the face from the sharp sting of the pellets, the people wear wire masks such as the one illustrated below. The vendors wander through the crowds carrying wire mesh masks in baskets and the harried spectators are more than glad to pay for protection.

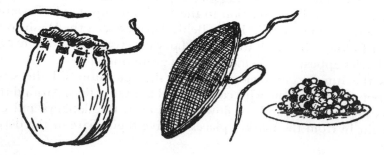

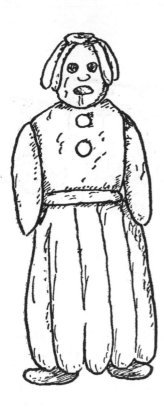
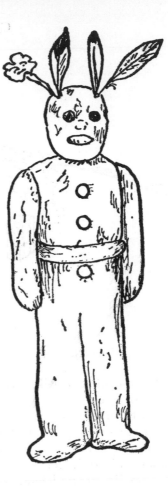

Festival of the Alban Hills

Twice a year, at Easter and in the fall, Genzanno and other small Italian villages bordering on the lake region of the Alban Hills hold a festival. It is an ancient pagan custom of blessing the vineyards in the spring and giving thanks for the harvest in the fall.

A part of the program that will interest children are the huge cakes that are given away to the guests. They are cut into grotesque figures and crudely decorated with rolls of dough to form the hair, skirts and other features. Feathers or flowers are forced into the top of the head and pepper beans inserted for eyes and buttons. A bright red pepper is used to make a mouth.

Surprisingly, the cookies are not made for eating since the dough is filled with bits of straw and an extra amount of salt. People take them home and use them as a *cookie barometers* in their cottages. If there is moisture in the air, the cookie becomes soft and it is going to rain.

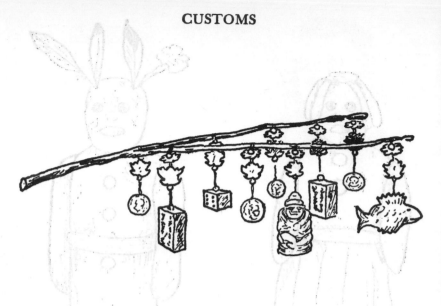

Friendship Branch

In Japan, a friend will present a friendship branch to another as a symbol of good wishes for all good things in life. The branch is twelve or fourteen inches long with several shoots or twigs left along the center stem as shown in the illustration. At intervals are attached small pink cherry blossoms which represent spring and gaiety to the Japanese. The ornaments attached vary in accordance with the wishes or personality of the friend that is to receive it. For instance, wishes on the branch above can be interpreted as follows: Fish or symbol of food, so the wish is for a bountiful harvest or storehouse of food. Buddha or a God to keep evil from the home. Dice, a good luck charm of chance. Money, many gold coins are hung from all the branches. Other symbols that can represent more intimate wishes for a friend, husband, wife or child may be used or ones that fit a particular talent or profession. The making of a friendship branch is an excellent craft for fellow campers.

Figure 1.   **Figure 2.**

Hawaiian Leis

The Hawaiian leis signify many things, all of which convey a message of special recognition. For instance, a man may present a lei to his sweetheart to express his love for her. A guest may receive a lei upon arrival or be presented with one of clove flowers as he departs. The clove flowers convey a special message of hope for a speedy return. Often a neighbor will hang a lei around the neck of another upon bringing a message of good news.

There are two types of leis, both of which are easily made:

Paper Lei (*Figure 1*). This lei is used at festivals or for large group gatherings to add gaiety and color much as we employ balloons or confetti. Cut small circles from crepe paper and pull edges with fingers to make them ruffled. String them on a piece of cord. Make several inches of one color circles, then make a section of another color. These may be alternated or many colors may be used. Many shades of one color may also be used.

Flower Lei (*Figure 2*). Each island in Hawaii has its own lei of all its native flowers. A flower lei is made by using heavy cord for the center. The cord is covered by sewing heads of flowers on all four sides until it is completely hidden.

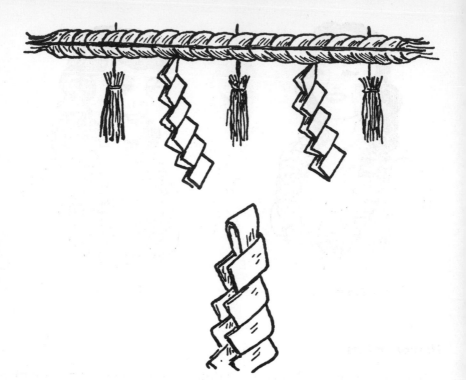

Shimes

Paper shimes are most important in a Japanese home because of their significance. They have a two-fold purpose, one to denote cleanliness and the other to ward off evil spirits and against dirt and filth. These pieces of folded paper are hung in private homes, particularly in the kitchen and over the pots and pans.

The papers are cut into rectangles and then folded in half so they can be laced together as shown above. They are then attached to a piece of new straw rope which is also a symbol of purity. The formal way of hanging the straw rope is to place the first woven portion on the right hand facing an object to be attached, because the left side is considered to be higher in rank than the right. It is made of clean straw. Between are hung three straws and two papers to represent the three karmas. The fact that the end of the straw is never cut off or woven in but left as it was signifies simplicity and cleanliness.

Figure 1. Wooden Toy Figures.

6. *Folk Toys*

FOLK TOYS are hard to find because they were fragile and broken in play. As the city grew close to rural homes, the peasant bought commercial toys for his children and turned his efforts to more useful occupations. Nurenburg, Germany, became the center of toy making because it was situated in the forest regions and the peasants spent the long winter evenings carving toys from wood to be sold in the spring. Germany is still the toy center and the mechanical devices and peasant figures are admired by the whole world.

Every boy that ever lived has been interested in soldiers so we find toy heroes dressed in gay uniforms in each country. Tradition has it that tin soldiers appeared during the reign of Frederic the Great.

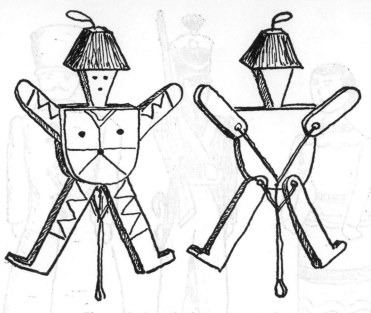

Figure 2. Detail of Jumping Jack.

Jumping Jacks

This type of toy is associated more often with England, although Jumping Jacks were also made in Germany and other European countries. There is a subtle humor or satire to pulling a string and making a figure jump, particularly if it is a policeman or soldier who is always making other people jump!

Figure 3 shows a typical Jumping Jack figure. It might have been made from cardboard or thin wood, but features were painted on with a brush. The arms, legs and head were cut separately and then fastened to the body by means of a clip or short string. To each appendage was fastened a string that led to the center back of the figure and which, in turn, was fastened to a longer string with a ring at the bottom end (see Figure 2). By pulling down on the ring, the arms and legs were caused to move. This folk toy brought laughter either to the very young who watched the movement, or to an adult who enjoyed the humor as suggested above.

Merry Jacks as shown in Figure 4 were animals that moved mechanically up and down a stick. Study the illustrations and you will know how they work.

Figure 3. Soldier Jumping Jack.

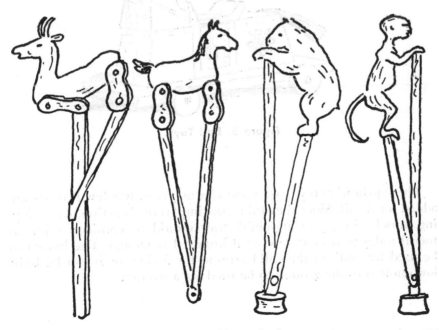

Figure 4. Merry Jacks.

Figure 5. Pull Toys.

These primitive toys have great charm, yet only a few features are added for detail. Since they fulfill the important function of developing muscles in a growing child, they should be considered just as useful today as they were several hundred years ago. The horse can be used for pulling the child around for a ride, or it can be built low enough to the ground to be used for a scooter.

Figure 6. Krusne Hory Toy.

This is one of the famous Krusne Hory toys. It is a symbol of the peasant's desire, a horse, and it was made to rock to attact the eye of the little ones. These toys were made of wood and often decorated in the royal colors.

Figure 7. Japanese Dolls.

These are traditional Japanese dolls made of wood and painted in bright, gay colors. Some had separate heads and were attached with a rubber band so they could be turned in different directions. In Europe, this type of doll was hollowed out in the center and used as salt and pepper shakers after it was discarded as a toy.

Figure 8. The swaddling clothes on these dolls were decorated with embroidery and beads. The Italians made them to represent the bambino, but in Germany, they had no religious significance and were used as dolls.

Figure 9. These are typical English dolls. The rag doll was made for small children and had few details as to features or clothing. It was customary to dress dolls in adult clothing more so than in other countries.

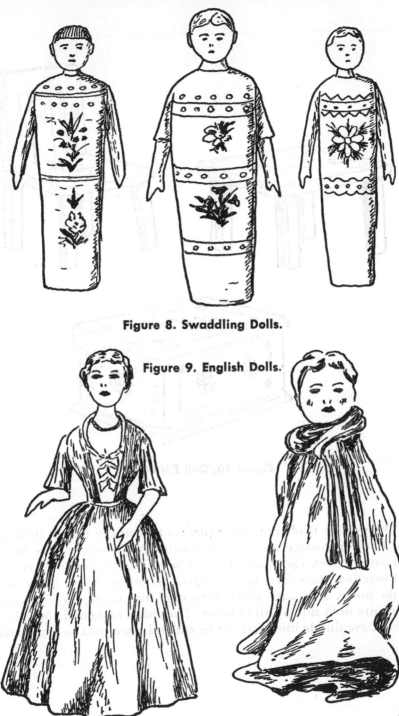

Figure 8. Swaddling Dolls.

Figure 9. English Dolls.

Figure 10. Doll Furniture.

The peasant made miniature pieces of furniture for his little girl, but since his cottage was sparsely furnished, the pieces were limited to chairs, tables, chests and beds. The wood was carefully cut and put together, then decorated in native designs to match other pieces in the home. This same idea can be used for making larger pieces of furniture to fit into a child's room. The chair, table and chest shown above have simple lines that can be cut and assembled by an amateur.

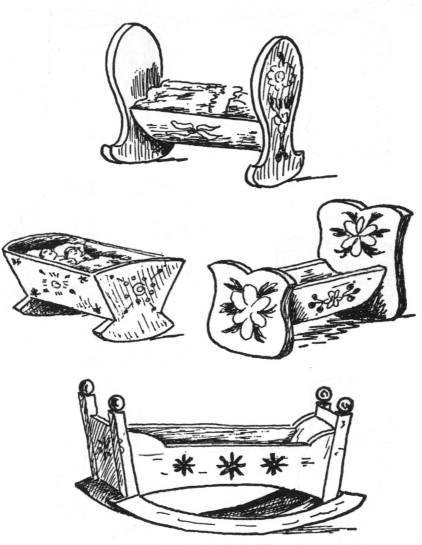

Figure 11. Doll Cradles.

A cradle for a doll was a favorite plaything. They were made of wood and decorated in peasant designs to match other furniture in the house. These are typical cradles made in central Europe.

Figure 12. Doll Dishes.

These little dishes were made from clay, fired and glazed in the same manner as were adult pots and vessels. Temporary dishes were perhaps made by the child itself, but they were not preserved for posterity. The making of play dishes is an excellent project for a child today since clay can be fired in a home kiln.

**Figure 13.
Apple Dolls.**

These character dolls are made by using a dried apple as a head and wire armature for the body. Select a medium sized apple, pare it and sculpture so that eye sockets, nose and mouth are indicated and place in a warm place to dry. When the head is dry, add features with colors on the face and use small beads for eyes. A peasant head dress may take the place of a wig. Fasten the head to the wire body armature and then wrap the arms, legs and body with rags until all are in correct proportion. Dress in native costumes.

Toy Village

From Germany and Italy come little wooden villages with fifty or more pieces tied together in a gold gauze bag. Among the pieces will be all types of cottages, trees, market places and stores. Animals of every size and description are also included. The very elaborate collections have inhabitants of the village and even go so far as to define an occupation such as cobbler, baker, char-woman, soldier, policeman, etc. In Germany the village is taken out at Christmas time and the figures set on mounds of cotton to make a snow scene for the window.

In order to cut a number of pieces the same shape and size, a long piece of wood was sculptured as shown in Figure 14. An outline of the article is sketched on one end, then the long edges are shaped according to the contours in the drawing. The wood is then cut into sections with a saw.

Figure 14. Detail Wood Block.

Figure 15. Toy Village Figures.

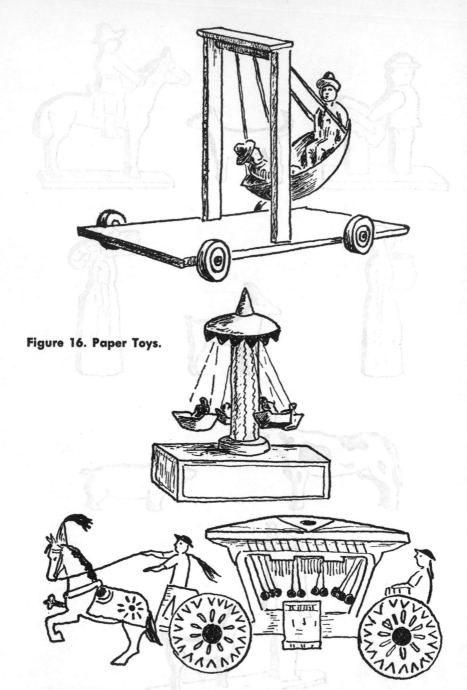

Figure 16. Paper Toys.

Here are some examples of toys that can be made of paper, or they can be made partly with paper and combined with wood. They are decorated in gay poster colors.

Figure 17. Vegetable Toys.

These are temporary toys that are useful for entertaining a child while his span of interest is short in duration. Potatoes seem to be the favorite vegetable for a body, yet turnips and carrots were also used. A few feathers, sticks or seeds add features and animate the toy.

Figure 18. Animated Rooster.

This toy rooster is made from stiff cardboard and, by cutting the head and tail separately, you can make them move when weight is swung. Enlarge the drawings in the above illustration, cut out each part, and then paint any color you desire for the rooster. Cut two pieces of string 7½" in length and attach one to neck and the other to tail. Now assemble parts and attach to body with paper staples, the kind that have a round head and two prongs that open outward. If you have an old wooden top, it will make an excellent weight. To bring the rooster to life, place him on a mantelpiece or table with a book serving as a weight on the projection (base), swing the top and he will move his head and tail.

Figure 19. Pecking Hens.

This is an early German mechanical toy, but it is still manufactured and sold today. It consists of a wooden platform on which are a number of hens, also made of wood. The heads are cut from separate pieces of wood and then fastened in a groove cut into the front of the body as shown in the illustration. They swing around on a nail that is driven through the breast of the hen and base of the neck. A string is attached to the base of each neck, brought down through a hole in the platform and tied to a center string about three inches below the base which holds them together. It in turn has a weight attached which, when swung around, causes the hens to peck on the board.

Figure 20. Mechanical Toys.

The Germans are most famous for making mechanical toys. Many of the fine examples came from the Black Forest region where the peasant made them during the long winter evenings. Mechanical toys are undoubtedly a thing of the past with electrical devices to take their place.

Figure 21. Wooden Birds.

Here are a number of versions of wooden birds, favorite subject for a folk toy. The rooster comes from Sweden and the others from central Europe. Bird whistles were made from wood or clay, using the tail as a mouthpiece. Examples are shown elsewhere in this book.

Figure 22. Doll Houses and Market Place.

Figure 23. Noah's Ark.

Here is an Italian model of a Noah's Ark with some of the inhabitants. Of course, the animals were in pairs and Noah's family included his wife and three sons and their wives. The ark itself is used for storing the figures when not in use.

Figure 24. Japanese Doll and Headgear.

This little Japanese doll was in a small wooden box with shelves on one side. On the shelves were beautifully made wigs that were to be used on different festival occasions in Japan. The head was made of porcelain and the body dressed in a silk kimono. This same idea can be used for peasant head dresses. Dress the body in a full skirt, plain blouse and shawl.

Figure 25. Nest of Dolls.

These wooden dolls are hollow inside and one is made a little smaller than the next. This is so all can fit inside the largest doll when not in use.

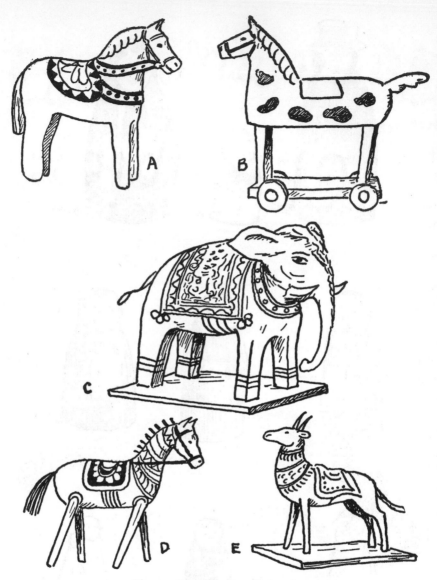

Figure 26. Wooden Animals.

Animals carved from wood always appeal to a small boy. The folk animal toys usually represented a favorite character in a folk tale or legend. The ones illustrated above are from:

A. Sweden   C. India

B. England   D and E. Asia

7. Crafts for Other Uses

Holidays

Every country celebrates it's own national holidays, but there are certain customs that are celebrated by Christians all over the world. Among these, of course, are Christmas and Easter. Then there are the festivals that originated centuries ago with the Druids and Pagans which have to do with the different seasons and the worship of the sun and moon. These are the most colorful of all celebrations and the source of many folk songs and dances.

Valentine's Day

St. Valentine, they say, was a grave and earnest Bishop, who was put to death in Rome on the fourteenth of February about the year 270 A.D. When he was canonized, the day of the month on which he died was dedicated to him. It is the time when young men and women send their love in the form of Valentines or illuminated love letters.

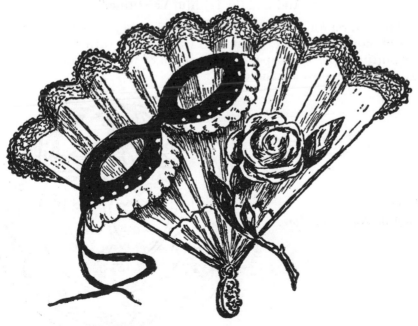

Figure 1. Napoleon's Valentine to Josephine.   213

Figure 2. Lace Valentine.

Next comes the hand-colored Valentines with lace edges as illustrated in Figure 2. The favorite decorations were motifs of hearts, flowers, hand with a bird carrying a message such as:

"Dearest say you will be mine
And wed thy faithful Valentine."

The fashion for small Valentines with movable heads after the manner of monkey on a stick came into vogue at the turn of the century. By putting a piece of paper at the bottom of the valentine, the heads were made to move up and down.

**Figure 3.
English Valentine Plate.**

214

Figure 4. Illuminated Love Letter.

The earliest Valentines on record are in manuscript form with colored heads, circles, squares and other designs around which messages were written. The writing was sometimes in elaborate scroll work which meant turning the valentine around and around an enormous number of times before the message was read.

Figure 4 shows an illuminated letter elaborately decorated with hearts and flowers all painted on by hand. The valentine itself is a cut paper design as you can see. The paper was folded into a square and one-fourth of the design (two hearts) traced in one corner. A sharp pair of scissors is used to cut out the design, being sure to cut through all four layers at the same time. When the paper is unfolded, it becomes a circle of hearts.

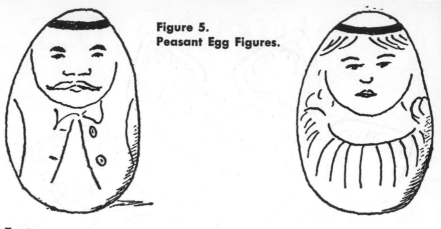

**Figure 5.
Peasant Egg Figures.**

Easter

Everywhere on Easter children play with eggs; some are colored while others are decorated in beautiful folk designs and still others are only imitations made of sugar or wood. In the Slavic countries, they take particular delight in embellishing them with mottos or wise sayings. We wish we could relate all the games and customs associated with this holiday but we must limit our space to some of the processes used in decorating the eggs.

Before the eggs are decorated, they must be either hard boiled or the yolks and egg whites removed from the shells. To do this, make a small hole at the top and bottom of the egg, then put the lips to the top hole and blow gently and steadily until all the contents are removed.

If you want to make party favors, you might try your hand at making peasant figures out of eggs as shown in Figure 5.

Figure 6. Eggs with Peasant Headdresses.

Figure 7. Decorations Made with Wax and Dye.

Several methods are employed in decorating eggs other than using a straight dye. The most satisfying method is to decorate them in colorful folk designs as shown in Figure 8. To do this, divide the surface of the egg into areas and select a motif that can be shaped to fit into the given spaces.

The eggs shown in Figure 7 were dipped into wax or paraffin and allowed to dry. The design is applied by cutting motifs out of the paraffin and scratching fine lines with a needle or sharp instrument. The egg is then placed in a dye bath and allowed to remain until desired color is attained. Heat the paraffin to remove it and polish the egg with oil.

Figure 8. Easter Eggs from Czechoslovakia.

Figure 9. Top of May-pole.

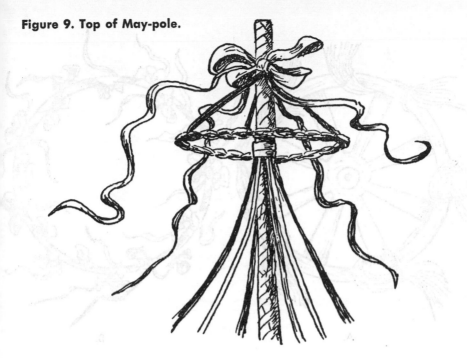

May-day

May-day is one of the holidays still being celebrated which was originated by the Pagans centuries ago. It is in England that the first day of May is a festival full of fun for the children as they welcome the coming of spring. A May Queen is crowned with flowers and children go to the woods to gather them and put them in specially made baskets. These they hang on a neighbor's door knob. Yet, as an old writer said "Their chiefest jewel is their May-pole."

In olden times, the May-poles were painted in alternate stripes of yellow and black, but today a white pole is used. Tack the ends of various colored ribbons (they should be a yard longer than the pole), at the top of the pole and suspend a wreath of flowers as shown in Figure 9. Decorate the extreme tip of the pole with gaily colored streamers or small flags.

An even number of persons are required for the dance; half the number takes the ribbon in the right hand and half in the left; they then face alternately right and left. When the dance commences, each dancer facing the right passes under the ribbon held by the one opposite facing the left; she then allows the next person going to the left to pass under her ribbon, and so on, tripping in and out, under and over until the ribbons are woven around the pole. Reverse the procedure to unwind the pole.

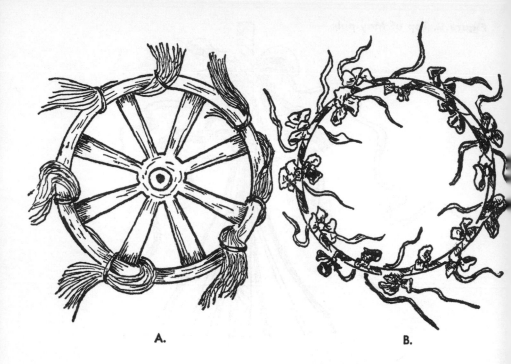

A.   B.

Figure 10. Wheels of Fortune.

The longest day of the year, June 21, is celebrated as Midsummer Eve in many European countries. Years ago, the Pagans celebrated this day with rejoicing because the sun stayed in the heavens longer than on any day of the year. In Sweden and Norway the season is symbolized by rolling great wooden wheels down the hillsides, sometimes attaching straw to the outer circle and setting fire to it at night, making a miniature midnight sun as it dashes down the steep incline. Figure 10A.

Other Wheels of Fortune were also symbols of the sun. They were made something like the one illustrated in Figure 10B and were used in two ways—one, it was wheeled "away" from you thus taking away your misfortunes, or it can be wheeled "toward" you,

> "Bringing happiness, fame, power and wealth
> True love, long life, good friends and health."

A fortune wheel can be made after your own fancy if you want to use them as a party favor or present one to a friend. Just tie symbols or good luck tokens around the rim, or decorate it with flowers and streamers.

220

Christmas

In America, Christmas is the greatest holiday of the year when all families gather together to give gifts to their loved ones and friends. The celebration follows very much the customs of an Old English Christmas of Santa Claus, lighting a Christmas tree, singing carols, lighting a yule log, etc. However, there are many charming old world customs that might be incorporated into an American Christmas and they are as follows:

Figure 1. Romanian Christmas Star.

Romania has a custom at Christmas when young boys walk through the streets singing carols and carrying a "Star of Bethlehem." This depicts the Holy Family on the eve of Christ's birth. It is a large wooden star covered with gold paint and decorated with paper frills and shiny beads and jewels.

The star is supported on a long pole and one of the boys carries it in the procession. Sometimes bells and ribbons are used to make the star even more beautiful and a candle placed inside to make it look like a heavenly lantern.

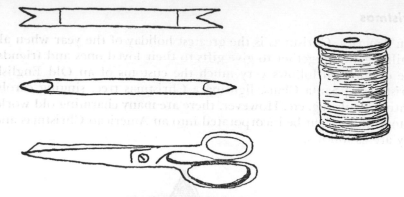

Figure 2. Tools for Straw.

The straw toys of Sweden were made with as much pride in their craftsmanship as the carvings the peasants made for their homes. In recent years, they have designed straw ornaments for export to this country at Christmas time and the highlights in the straw make them gleam on a Christmas tree. We have selected the Christmas objects to illustrate because they suit our subject, but many other items are made, such as the heart and horse shoe shown in Figure 3.

To make strawcraft quite successful, the workmanship must be carefully executed. First, the straws should be matched as to size and color. The items we have seen were made from small, very firm stalks such as wheat or rye and gold in color. The ends were carefully notched or cut on a slant as shown in Figure 2. You need a pair of small, sharp scissors to do this work.

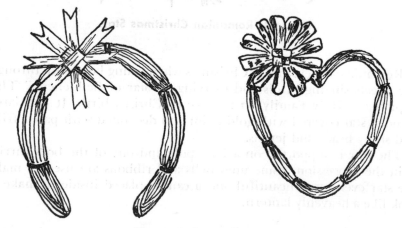

Figure 3. Straw Favors.

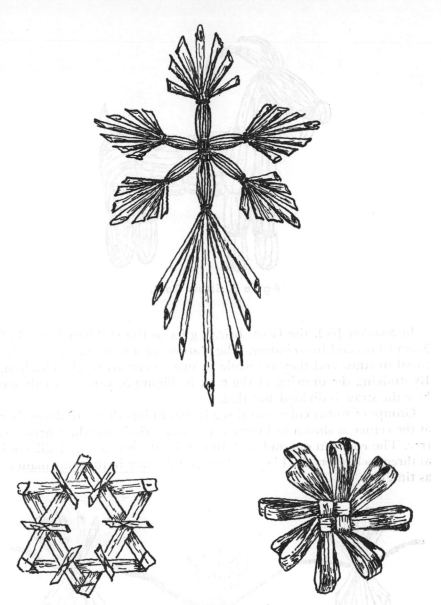

Figure 4. Christmas Stars.

There are many versions of the star to be found; no doubt it is because the straws can be bent into so many different shapes they become a problem for the designer. The stalks are lashed into place with a thin red cord at cross points. Note the straws in one star are held in place with a square weave of soft straw.

223

Figure 5. Straw Goat.

In Sweden Jöel, the Goat, brings gifts to the children instead of Santa Claus and his reindeer. The features of a goat are easily sculptured in straw and they are made in many versions by the children. By studying the drawing of the goat in Figure 5, you can easily see how the straw is divided and tied.

Groups of straws cut about three inches in length are tied together at the center as shown in Figure 6 to form a chain for the Christmas tree. The ends fan out and each bunch is attached to a red silk cord at three-inch intervals. They are hung on the tree in the same manner as tinsel.

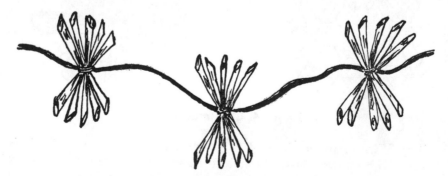

Figure 6. Straw Garland.

These illustrations show how figures are constructed from straw. Wet the straw if it needs to be bent into shape and sew with a fine thread at intervals. The maiden is made by tying enough straws together to form the head. The straws are then divided into three parts at the neck to form waist and two arms. Tie a string at the waist line and flare out the straws to form a skirt. Insert enough new straws to form a hollow skirt.

Figure 7. Straw Angel.

Figure 8. Snow Maiden.

The Nativity

This particular Nativity scene came from Germany and, because the figures have so much appeal, we have tried to duplicate them with exact drawings. The Germans have emphasized the making of crèches more than most countries because they like to fit them into a snow setting for a window decoration during the Holidays. Many scenes are very elaborate with water wheels, skating ponds and sometimes whole villages.

If these figures had been made fifty years ago, they undoubtedly would have been carved from wood. However, these were made of white plastic and costumes added with red, blue, green and gold paint. The same figures can be most effective modeled from clay and decorations added with under glazes. Note that the individual characters are attached to a flat base so that they can stand alone.

Figure 9. Two Crèches from Oberammergau, Germany.

Figure 10. The Pinata.

In Mexico, the children receive their gifts on Christmas from a huge jar, or Pinata, such as the one shown above. It is like a grab bag hung from the ceiling and is filled with oranges, sweets, or little gifts suitable for anyone fortunate enough to pick it up from the floor. The children strike it with sticks or canes until the jar breaks and then there is a wild scramble to pick up the gifts as they fall to the floor. Since jars are made in great abundance in Mexico, no one minds when one is broken.

Figure 11. Christmas Cookies.

In Norway, and other northern countries, many cookies are made and decorated with care. Every child has his "pile" of cookies on Christmas Eve, each of which has some significance. The cookies shown in the above illustration were shaped in a wooden mold decorated with incised cuts.

Figure 12. Apple Jack-o-Lanterns.

All-Hallow Eve

The ancient Celts celebrated the first of May for sowing; the solstice on the twenty-first of June for ripening and the eve of the first of November for harvesting. Of the three, only Halloween is celebrated in America. It is an evening full of superstitious fun with pranks from children and the youth playing games by which their future might be read.

It is in Ireland where this is considered the best evening of the year for the practice of magic and witchcraft. The children carry little lanterns with grotesque faces to ward off the evil spirits. In this country we have the pumpkin jack-o-lanterns, but in Ireland they are made of apples. The center is hollowed out, then eyes, nose and mouth are cut as shown in Figure 12. They are, of course, illuminated with a candle.

Figure 13. Wedding Certificate.

It is the custom in many European countries to decorate a wedding or birth certificate in folk designs as shown in the two illustrations. Parchment, or a good quality of paper, is used for the background and the names are framed at the center with a heart or flowers. Often some of the family history is injected into the design by adding a crest or a picture of a legend.

Birth Certificate.

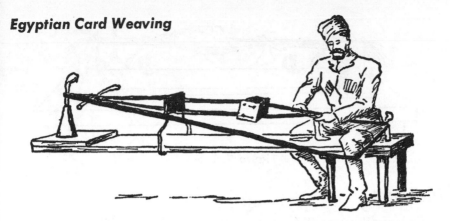

From the Middle East comes this fascinating craft, card weaving. It is a special technique requiring simple equipment which can be easily made or improvised, once you have caught the idea. Archaeologists found in several Egyptian tombs sets of thin tablets or cards made of horn. These tablets were perforated in the corners and contained curious markings and it was concluded there must have been a game played with them. Finally, in one tomb, a complete tablet weaving apparatus was discovered set up as if for use, and holding a partly finished girdle, with cards threaded with brightly colored strands. From this discovery, craftsmen were able to figure out one of our most interesting weaving techniques for making gay peasant belts, ties, headbands, etc. Since it requires about twenty cards for each width woven, the width is limited to two or three inches as the cards must be held in the hands in order to change sheds as shown in figure 1.

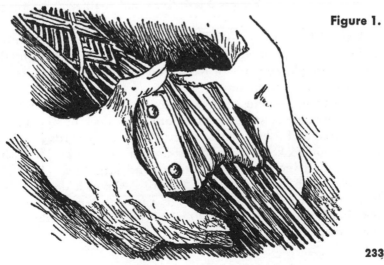

Figure 1.

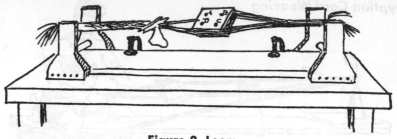

Figure 2. Loom.

Equipment

First of all, you will want to gather together the necessary equipment which will include the cards, shuttle, scissors, etc. The warp must be fastened at both ends to horizontal bars which will hold it steady and taut as you work. The frame illustrated in Figure 2 can be made very cheaply and we recommend that you make one if possible. It is clamped onto a table while in use with two C-clamps.

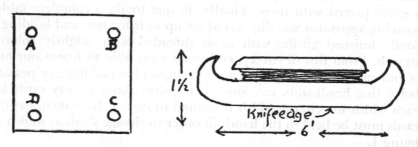

Figures 3 & 4. Card and Shuttle.

A small flat shuttle, Figure 4, six to eight inches long and an inch and a half wide, is used for carrying the weft and for beating the work. Shuttles should be made of hard wood and well sandpapered so they will not rough up the warp.

You can make your own cards or buy them at a handicraft shop. They are made of smooth cardboard, or a deck of playing cards can be squared and used to advantage. Measure the cards into three inch squares and make as many cards as you need. The holes should be about a half inch from the corners and large enough to allow the thread to slip through easily. Figure 3 shows a detail of the card. Note that the holes are lettered A,B,C, and D, clockwise. The A position is usually the control or key position, from which you count the turn of the cards.

234

Materials

Mercerized cotton crochet and knitting yarns are the best to use for card weaving. Carpet warp is sufficient for your first experiment as it is cheap and good for trying out designs and colors. Examples of fine Arabian and Persian work in museums are made of silk warp shot with silver and gold threads.

The ply of the thread and the number of cards determine the width of the work. Twenty cards threaded with number five pearl cotton will make a strip about one and one-half inches wide. Bright high colors and bold designs are most effective.

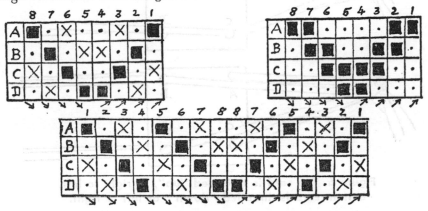

Figure 5. Graph of Pattern.

First of all, you will want to make a graph of your pattern. This is done by drawing four rows of squares as indicated in the above graph and indicating the color of thread to be used in each square. Each of the four rows represents the four holes in each card, A B C or D. You can use different symbols in each square to indicate different colors. You are now ready to thread your cards.

Measure off your warp threads, laying them carefully across the table, the colors separate. The graph shows how many threads of each color must be measured off. Allow three times the finished length, plus six or eight inches extra for tying the warp to the frame. Follow the diagram for threading the cards, laying them face up, one on the other in order as you thread them. Draw the thread through evenly, leaving a shorter length, about eighteen inches, on the left hand side. Card number one should be on the bottom when you have finished. Note that the pattern always repeats itself from the center of the belt out to the border. It is better, therefore, to thread two cards at a time with the same colors and stack them in two piles to be attached later to the loom for weaving.

235

How to Thread Cards

You will note small arrows at the bottom of the graphs shown in Figure 5. Part are pointing up and the others are pointing down. This means that the cards designated by the square must be threaded either "up" or "down." All threading is from the face side of the cards, however.

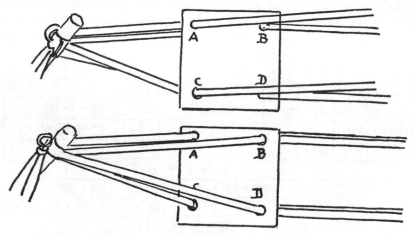

**Figure 6. Top card is threaded "up", or right to left.
Bottom card is threaded "down", or left to right.**

When "up" is indicated, hold your thread in your right hand and let it run that way. For the down threading, hold your thread in your left hand and let it run in that direction. It is a little difficult for a beginner to understand the difference in threading up and down but it does make a difference in your pattern. Each single card must have the threads running the same way or weaving would be impossible.

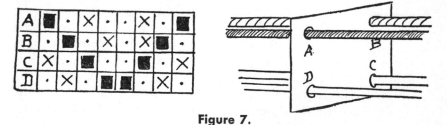

Figure 7.

Now let's take graph No 1 in Figure 5 and see how to thread the cards. This unit calls for eight black threads, eight red (squares with X) and sixteen white (squares with dot). Card No 1 would call for one black strand, one red and two white. The arrow at the bottom indicates that it is threaded "up" so you would thread right to left.

How to Weave

When the cards are all ready, straighten out the warp with your fingers at the shorter end. It is good to fasten the cards together with an elastic band while you are doing this. When the warp on the left hand side is straight, tie it onto one of the bars of the loom. Now straighten out the other threads and tie them fast, having them very taut. The cards should be in the center of the warp and should move freely back and forth.

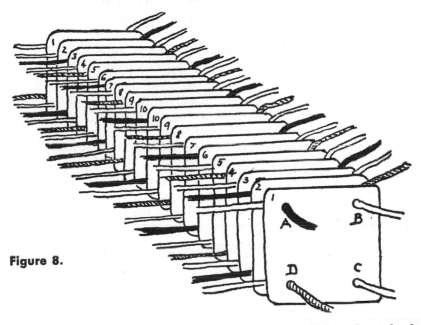

Figure 8.

The illustration above shows the cards threaded and ready for weaving. Note that the cards are numbered 1—10 and then the same numbers are repeated from the center on out. This is because the design is reversed on the second half so it is easier to keep track of your cards by threading two at a time.

You will need four tongue depressors or four pieces of cardboard of about the same size for shed sticks. These will help straighten the warp during the first three operations and keep the edges straight.

If your cards are properly set up and your warp even you will have a clear shed. Put the first depressor in the shed at the left as near the bar as possible, and give the cards one turn to the left, from "A" position to "B" position. Put in your second spreader, again as far to the left as it will go, and give another turn, and so on until you have marked all your sheds. Now you are ready to weave.

Your shuttle should be wound with enough weft for the whole piece. The weft should be the color of the border, so that it will not show. It is a good idea to have the border a solid color to frame the pattern.

Grasp the cards in both hands as shown in Figure 1 and give your cards a turn from "A" position to "B" position. Bring your shuttle through the new shed and beat your work well. Make another turn of the cards, and put in another shot of weft, and so on until you have returned to the "A" position. Now reverse, and weave in the opposite direction for four turns. Continue this process until your strip is finished. Each time you draw your weft through, put your shuttle into the new shed in the opposite direction, ready for the next turn of the cards. Then pull the weft through using your two hands before beating your work.

If your warp becomes too tight or too slack, you can undo it at the right hand side and adjust it. Your weaving will come up on the left hand side. Beat your work well after each shot of weft. This makes it smooth and even. Try to turn your cards all at once by placing the palm of your right hand under them and shifting them gently. If any of the cards stick, use your fingers to right them.

The customary way of weaving is to make four turns one way and four turns back to the original position. This is the Egyptian technique and your warp will never become twisted. However, some of the patterns call for turning the cards by different schemes of rotation. Try making one strip with, first, the four turns each way. Now turn several cards one or two turns, and then put your shuttle through, noting the effect on your pattern. In this way, you will learn how to graph designs and how to arrange colors for any desired effect. Yet there is always the element of surprise and suspense to urge you on. When you have created a design worthy of repetition, be sure to attach a sample of your graph for identification.

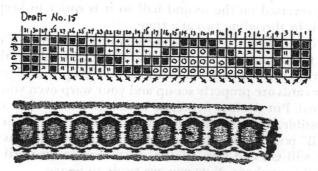

Draft No. 15

Figure 9. Graph with Design.

238

Varying Patterns Without Shifting Cards

The upper four patterns resulted when the reversing took place on the four different letters. The relative position of the cards themselves was not changed. A given warping permits four patterns formed by reversing on different letters.

Variations by Shifting Cards

Countless other variations could be made by changing the position of the cards themselves. For instance, after weaving several inches with a twenty-two card pattern, shift cards 3, 4, 5, and 6 on both sides one turn to the right. Then weave an inch more to see the resulting pattern. Then turn the same eight cards once to the left, their original position, and make one more turn to the left and see how that effects the pattern. There is hardly any limit to the possible patterns that may be tried out by variations with a given original warping.

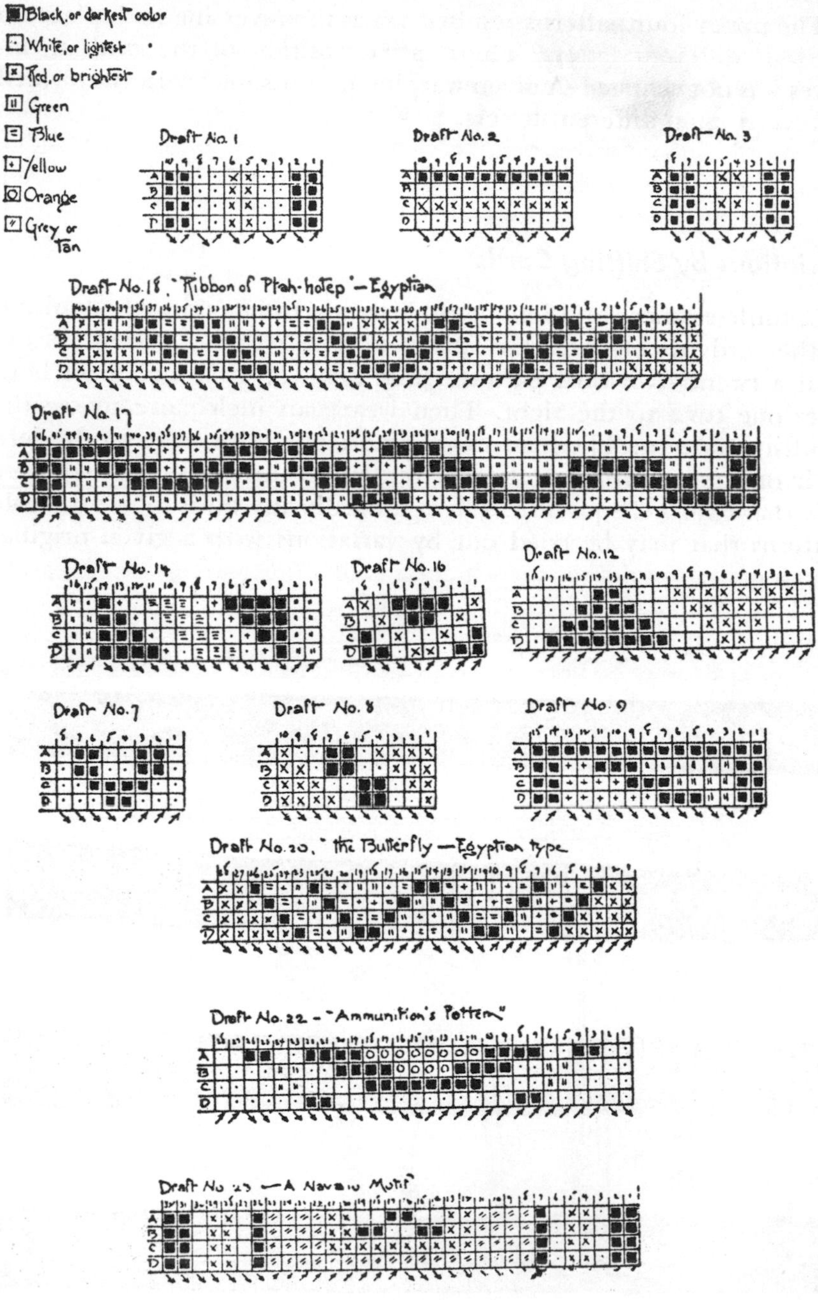

Black, or darkest color
White, or lightest •
Red, or brightest •
Green
Blue
Yellow
Orange
Grey or Tan

Draft No. 1
Draft No. 2
Draft No. 3

Draft No. 18. "Ribbon of Ptah-hotep" — Egyptian

Draft No. 17

Draft No. 14
Draft No. 16
Draft No. 12

Draft No. 7
Draft No. 8
Draft No. 9

Draft No. 20. "the Butterfly — Egyptian type

Draft No. 22 - "Ammunition's Pattern"

Draft No. 23 — A Navajo Motif

Mosaics

Since mosaics has become the latest and most popular craft in ' United States, we are going to give detailed instructions for various techniques, as there are few books on the subject. It is ' to be a popular and lasting craft because it can be applied to so m. uses, both indoors and outside the house. Also, the laying of mosaics is so simple it can be enjoyed by the beginning craftsman and even children can make small projects.

Mosaics is perhaps the oldest craft known to man, with examples dating back to 3500 B.C. The earliest mosaics were laid by the Egyptians whose classic expressions were in the form of geometric patterns of design, perfect for this technique. The Romans introduced the use of colored glass and used it in designs to decorate public buildings while, heretofore, mosaics were used chiefly for floors in Greece and Egypt. In the Italian churches was where the craft reached its highest degree of perfection. The great artists built murals of gold leaf and departed from the formal geometric designs and gave detailed features to figures of the Holy Family and saints of the Church. For many years mosaics, as an art medium, almost disappeared except in Mexico and parts of South America where they are used to decorate buildings and market places. Now, with its sudden revival, this ancient craft may be here to stay. The designs and texture of the tiles blend so well with our modern furniture and, as you will see later on in this chapter, there are many projects that can lighten the work of the housewife.

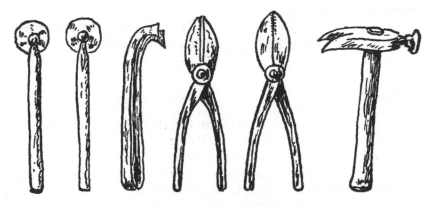

Figure 1. Mosaic Tools.

Figure 2. Mosaic Materials.

In order to satisfy both the unskilled and creative craftsman, we are going to describe two methods of laying mosaics. The first, or creative method, is used in Italy and has been practised to a limited extent in this country. The second, or commercial method, has been worked out by manufacturers of tiles so that the mosaics are laid face up on the projects. Before trying your hand at this craft, read both directions carefully and perhaps you can combine the two.

Creative Mosaics

Colored glass is the best medium for this type of mosaics—but pieces of china, pottery, or even shells can be used. In order to get started, you should buy several small tools including two good glass cutters, a dentist's tweezer, and two sturdy pliers, as shown in Figure 1. A small hammer is also useful. You will also need certain materials such as a piece of heavy wrapping paper, a jar of home-made flour paste and a flat board on which to build the design, Figure 2.

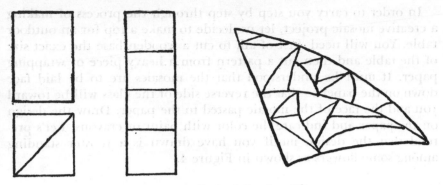

Figure 3. Method of Cutting Glass.

Glass is the most satisfactory medium to use for this creative type of mosaics since it comes in every color and one can find a graduation of different shades which is important in carrying out a design. It also resists moisture, a quality one must consider when the project is to be used out of doors. To begin, you should collect glass in every hue and cut it into various shapes to be stored away in jars for future use. You can buy scrap glass by the bag from glass companies, or you can always find glass of sorts on your pantry shelves or around the neighborhood.

If you have pieces of colored glass large enough to break into sections, you should make the incision first with a glass cutter and then break apart with two pliers. Place them on either side of the cut and break the glass apart by holding the handles firmly in each hand and bear down gently until it breaks. Make your cutting lines irregular as shown in Figure 3 so that you will have small, odd-shaped, pieces to fill in the various areas. You will also want some square and rectangular pieces to fit into the background. If some of the pieces of glass are not suitable for cutting, you may break them apart with a hammer.

How to Plan a Mosaic Design

After you select a project, draw a design that will fit well into the background and cut your glass accordingly. It is very important to use three to five different shades of each color in order to give contrast and life to the mosaic. The Italians interspersed it with an occasional gold square to make it sparkle. We should also point out that in making your first creative mosaic, you should choose a project suitable for the out of doors as it will be cast in cement which is too heavy for household use.

In order to carry you step by step through the process of making a creative mosaic project, let us decide to make a top for an outdoor table. You will need, first of all, to cut a wooden base the exact size of the table and then cut a pattern from a heavy piece of wrapping paper. It must be understood that the mosaics are to be laid face down on the paper so that the reverse side of the glass will be toward you and the face of the mosaic pasted to the paper. Draw the design on the paper and indicate the color with paint or crayons. Let's pretend that the design motif you have drawn is a rooster standing among some flowers as shown in Figure 4.

Figure 4. Mosaic Rooster.

In order to make a colorful rooster, you should have glass in at least six shades of red, three shades of pink and if possible, some orange, purple and lavender. The bill and legs require yellow if you want to be realistic, and then an occasional gold and blue square will add interest or contrast to the design. The flowers can be made from any shade of glass you might have on hand, but you will need several shades of green, varying from greenish yellow to deep jade, for the foliage.

Before laying the mosaics, make some flour paste about the consistency of heavy cream for holding them in place. Then place the paper pattern on the foundation of the table and begin dipping the glass pieces into the paste and laying them in place on the design. If there is a blemish in the glass, be sure to keep it on top because you are working in reverse. Since you have several shades of red, place the darkest mosaics along the top of the rooster and graduate the colors throughout the body, using the pink ones for the breast and legs. Fit in an occasional blue or gold one where it will not interrupt the design. It is best to lay on the various pieces of glass before pasting them in place to see if you have enough of each color to carry out your plan.

Begin pasting the mosaics around the outline of the rooster first

244

and arrange the straight part of the glass pieces to point toward the outer edge. Do not arrange the mosaics edge to edge, but allow at least 1/16″ interval between as shown in Figure 5. This is very impor-

Figure 5. Mosaic Detail.

tant in order to have the glass entirely imbedded in the cement. Try to keep the spaces between as equal as possible. Careful workmanship will add to the finished design.

After all the mosaics have been laid in the rooster, place the paper pattern on the table you plan to use for casting the cement. Now arrange the mosaics in the flowers and foliage and try to think of other objects you might include to make an interesting composition. You can have just plain cement for the upper part of the background, or you may include such objects as pebbles, shells, colored stones, or you may paste on an occasional piece of colored glass. Just remember that the objects used need not be the same depth as the glass since the cement is to be poured over from the back. This is your first project so why not use a number of objects as an experiment. When you have pasted all the mosaic pieces in place as shown in Figure 6, you are ready to cast them in cement.

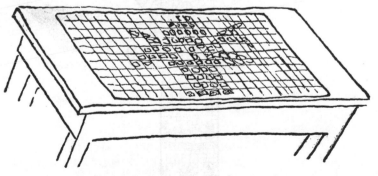

Figure 6. Mosaics Ready for Casting.

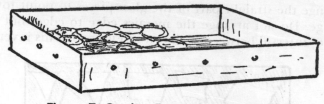

Figure 7. Casting Frame for Mosaics.

How to Cast Mosaics

When your design is completed and all of your pieces are pasted in place, your next problem is to cast them in cement. Since the project is an out-of-doors table, the top should be three to four inches thick according to the size of the block. It is necessary to make a casting frame the exact dimensions of the table top in order to hold the cement in place until it dries. The frame should be at least one inch higher than the expected block and across the center is tacked some chicken wire as shown in Figure 7. The wire must be placed in the frame so that the cement will cover it as it is poured, thus giving it support when dry.

Use Portland cement mixed with sand for the foundation. The proportion you use depends on the coarseness of the sand. Use three measures of sand to one of cement if sand is coarse, or five to one with very fine sand. Add enough water to make it the consistency of heavy cream. You may stir in some dry color if you want to tint it.

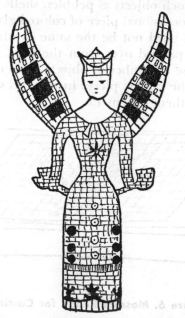

Creative Mosaic Designs.

Place the frame over the mosaic design and pour in the cement very slowly in order not to disturb the pieces pasted to the paper. In fact, it is a good idea to put in a thin layer first with a spoon and after it sets a little while, pour in the rest of the cement until you have the desired thickness. Be sure to cover the chicken wire so that it is approximately in the center of the block. Allow the cement to stand several days before removing the frame.

Now the exciting moment has arrived. Turn the table top over and remove the paper by soaking it in warm water to dissolve the paste. Clean the mosaics with a damp rag and remove extra pieces of cement around the edge with a small chisel. You are now ready to frame the edge of the table top, ideas for which you will find later on in this chapter.

Figure 8. Plaques from Prague Applied to Mosaic Designs.

Mosaics the Commercial Way

During the past year, mosaics has become a very popular craft, both with the professional craftsman and the hobbiest. The commercial artists have designed beautiful modern furniture decorated with this ancient craft, and every day a new use for mosaics is being discovered. This is partially due to the fact that commercial companies have recognized the possibilities of mosaics as a craft medium and have simplified the method of laying them. Now all the craft supply houses carry mosaic squares in beautiful colors and have worked out a way of laying them face side up, which certainly helped to popularize the craft.

In general, tiles are made in three media, glass, ceramic and porcelain. The glass and ceramic tiles usually measure 3/4" square and come in sheets containing 225 tiles. The porcelain tiles are approximately 3/8" square and are found in sheets of 625. All of the tiles are glued to a heavy paper and can easily be removed by soaking in warm water. It is possible to buy each type of tile in many beautiful colors from the very light to the deepest shades. Some companies manufacture vari-colored squares flecked with gold which give life and sparkle to a design. The ceramic and porcelain tiles come with unglazed edges so it is necessary to frame the finished project. Glass mosaics have a smooth beveled edge so the framing is not important.

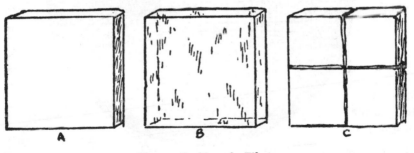

Figure 9. Mosaic Tiles.

A. Ceramic   B. Glass   C. Porcelain

As we stated before, these tiles are laid face up. First, decide on your project and make a foundation to which the tiles can be glued. Remember the porcelain and ceramic tiles have an unglazed edge so plan for a frame of some kind. Divide the area completely into small squares and, since the tiles are to be laid about 1/16" apart, make them a little larger than 3/4". Now block in a design by using crayons to indicate color and remember to include several shades of the same color to add interest. Also, add an occasional gold one as they do in Italy. You are now ready to set the tiles.

A dab of liquid adhesive is applied to the bottom of each tile which is set in place according to the squares in the design. Allow at least 1/16" space to remain between each tile to be filled in later with a form of cement called "grout." It is a white powder, part cement and marble dust, that becomes a heavy paste when mixed with water. It can be tinted with dry colors if you do not wish a white background. After the tiles are set and cement dried, rub the grout over the top until all spaces between are filled and clean off excess with a damp rag. The grout serves two purposes—it binds the tiles together and prevents moisture from seeping underneath.

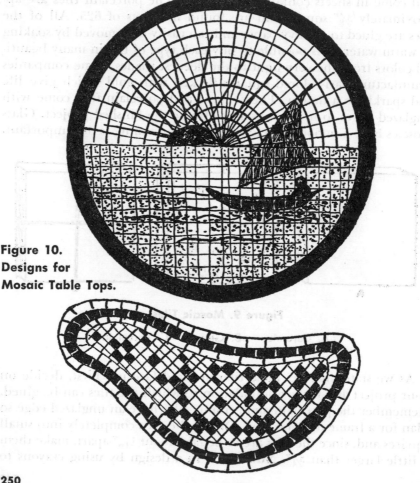

**Figure 10.
Designs for
Mosaic Table Tops.**

How to Finish Edges

If your mosaics are made of glass, you need not think of a special frame for the project. Ceramic and porcelain tiles are glazed only on the top so the white, raw edges require a treatment of some kind. The most satisfactory way is to continue laying the tiles down over

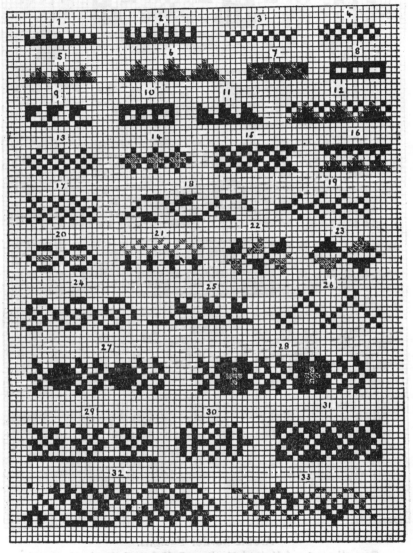

Arabic Border Designs.
Compliments of United Nations Relief and Works Agency.

the edge of the table and filling in the spaces with grout. Some craftsmen prefer a metal frame of chrome or copper. A simpler, and less expensive frame is a wooden molding the depth of the tile and attached to the extreme edges of the table.

Arabic Border Designs.
Compliments of United Nations Relief and Works Agency.

Toy Animals

From all parts of the world come these little animals made from wool or other native materials. They are, of course, used as a toy but they have other significant uses such as a token for keeping away evil spirits, symbol of a sacred animal, or identification with the folklore of a country.

Animals Made from Wool. These fluffy animals are made from knitting worsted or wool remnants and are easily shaped or sculptured to the desired form. However, burlap ravelings or fine grasses may also be used as we will explain later on. In general—the body, head and legs are made separately and the parts attached before the ends are clipped.

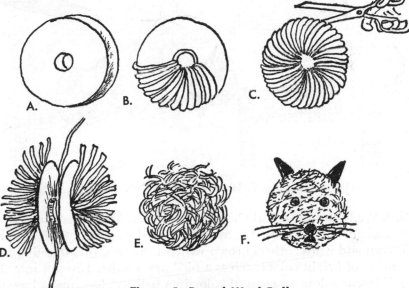

Figure 1. Round Wool Ball.

First, here is how to make a round ball from wool or string. Cut two identical cardboard discs the diameter you wish for the ball. Cut a hole in the center of each disc as shown in Figure 1A. Next, fit the discs together and begin winding by taking it through the hole, around the outer edge, then back through the hole. Continue until you have several layers, depending on the size yarns you are using, Figure 1B. When the surfaces of the discs are covered, scissors are inserted between them and the threads are cut all around the outer edge, Figure 1C. Now separate the two discs about 1/4 inch and wind a string around the wool between the two holes and tie with a secure knot. Leave at least two inches on either side of string for handling purposes, Figure 1D. Remove the cardboard discs by cutting them away and the wool will spring together to form a ball as shown in Figure 1E. You are now ready to sculpture it to the shape of an animal head by trimming with a pair of sharp scissors. Add ears, eyes and mouth as shown in Figure 1F.

Figure 2. Wool Bird and Cat.

Bird. We found these little birds in Germany. They are two inches long, made of varied colored yarn and the beak and tail of felt. Some are brown and white, others brown with a robin red breast and some were made of bright colors such as a bird never wore. It is possible to have different colors, or spots of color in a ball by changing colors of yarn while winding the disc. A large ball is used for the body and a small one for the head as shown in Figure 2. Use a piece of thin wire for the legs and feet and fasten it to the body by inserting it between the discs and bending it down on either side. Bend edge of wire to form feet as shown in the above illustration. Shape the head and add two small beads for eyes. The tail and beak can be cut from felt.

Cat. The body, legs and tail of a cat are made on a jig as shown in Figure 3. The head is made from a ball as shown in Figure 1. It is sculptured into a heart-shape and flattened in the front and back. Small green sequins make appropriate and amusing eyes for a cat, or you may use a glass bead. Make the ears of felt and embroider a mouth with thread in a contrasting color.

254

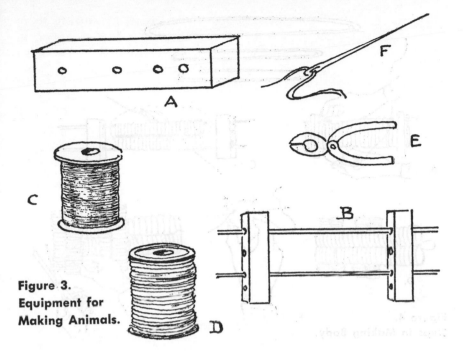

Figure 3.
Equipment for
Making Animals.

If you are going to make a number of wool animals, you will need a jig of some kind on which to wind the yarn and hold it in place while the center wire is being sewed in place. You must have two parallel bars that can be adjusted to different widths in order to make the body and legs. If you happen to have a frame for making hair-pin lace, which are sold in department stores, you may use it; otherwise you should make a jig as shown in Figure 3 A and B.

To make the frame, take two blocks of wood 1″ x 1″ x 4″ and drill a number of matching holes in each piece. Buy two metal rods about 10″ in length to form the two sides of the jig. The illustration shows how they can be inserted into different holes to attain various widths.

In addition to a jig, you will need a spool of thin wire to be used for the center of body and legs. If you have some wire in the house which can be easily bent, use it—otherwise, buy a spool of 18 gauge wire at the hardware store. It is good to have a pair of pliers for bending the wire but this is not essential. You will need a spool of heavy thread to match the yarn you are planning to use for the animal, and a needle large enough to receive the thread.

You are now ready to make an animal. Decide on the measurements of the body, legs and tail and remember the head is usually included in length of body. By inserting the metal rods in different combinations of holes, the space between the rods can be adjusted to make the different parts of the animal.

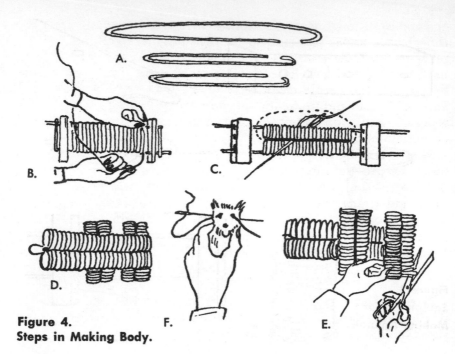

Figure 4.
Steps in Making Body.

The principle involved in making an animal is to have a central stem on which to fasten the yarn securely and then be able to bend it into different shapes. In order to do this, you must follow directions given below:

Step 1. Make a drawing of the animal and decide on measurements of legs, length and diameter of body, ears, etc. Cut a wire twice the length of the body and bend it in half as shown in Figure 4A. Note the wires come together about ½″ from one end, thus forming a loop at each extremity. Cut wires for legs and tail and bend in the same manner.

Step 2. Wind the yarn into two balls so you can wind it onto the jig by using two strands at a time. Wind it around and around the outside of the frame, back and forth, until you have approximately seven layers as shown in Figure 4B. This is called a pad. If you wish to use two or more colors, you can have one strand of one color and one of another which will give a mottled effect. Stripes may be made by alternating contrasting yarns during the winding but spots must be added after the winding and sewing is completed.

Step 3. You are now ready to sew the body wire onto the yarn pad. Lay the wire along the center and allow the two loops to extend just a little beyond the yarn at both ends. The tail will be attached later to one end and the tongue to the other. Thread a needle and tie thread to loop at one end and bring it underneath pad to opposite end and up through loop. Now bring the needle down and carry the thread back under pad and up through original loop and you are ready to sew. The sewing is very important as every strand of wool must be caught with the thread and fastened to the wire. This is done by pushing the needle down next to the wire—around the thread back of the pad and up beside the wire on the opposite side. This is repeated, sewing up and down, over the wire on top and over thread on bottom of the pad until they are completely covered with stitches.

Step 4. You are now ready to cut loops in both body and legs. Remove the pad and insert scissors as shown in Figure 4E. This is the most interesting part of the toy making because you bend the legs down and arrange the forepart of the pad to resemble a head. Work with it to give it animation and personality. Sculpture the various parts by using a pair of sharp scissors and be sure all the loops have been cut. The animal can be "fluffed" by running the teeth of the comb back and forth or crosswise through the yarn without removing it.

Step 5. Add eyes—shoe buttons for large animals and beads for smaller ones. Ears can be cut from felt, or you may make them on the jig as you did the tail and legs. See Figure 4F.

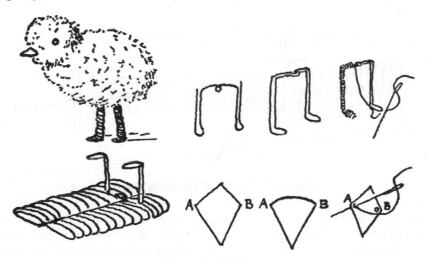

Figure 5. Chicken.

This little woolly chicken is made from a single wool pad as shown in the drawing. Make the legs of wire and shape the feet. If you like, you may cover the wire with thread by using a buttonhole stitch. Add beak and eyes and then fasten feet to a small stand cut from wood or cardboard.

Figure 6. Giraffe and Scottie.

Giraffe. To make a giraffe, cut three wires as follows: one for body 23″, one 10″ for front legs and another 10″ for hind legs. Bend all the wires in half as shown in Figure 3. The body presents a special problem in that the head, neck and body are different widths but made on the same central wire:

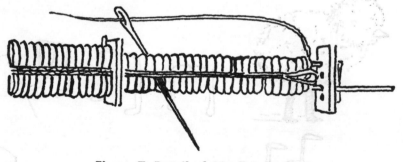

Figure 7. Detail of Giraffe's Body.

Study the above illustration which shows how it is possible to make the different widths. Remove the side rods after the wire has been sewed to the body pad, readjust the width and wind yarn to make neck and again sew on center wire. Remove rods again and make the head. Follow instructions given in Figure 3 for assembling body. Use very light corn-colored yarn with occasional shades of tan to give a mottled effect. Make ears of felt and the horns of wire which can be painted or wrapped with wool.

Scottie. This little dog can be made in any size but try cutting a body wire 9″ and leg wires 6″ and bending them in half. Make the body pad about two inches wide and 5/8" thick. Also, make three little pads about 3/4" long and as narrow as possible for the ears and tail. Follow directions given in Figure 3 for assembling body and cutting loops. Sew a red felt tongue to wire loop at one end and fasten tail to other. Use black shoe buttons for eyes and sew them to a tiny white felt pad. Trim to shape and add collar and blanket if you desire.

Figure 8. Camel and Panda.

Camel. This animal presents a special problem because a hump must be added to its back. Cut a body wire 10" long and two leg wires 8"; then bend them all in half. For the hump, cut a wire 5" long and bend to 2½". Use several shades of brown for making pads and follow directions given in Figure 3 for sewing on the wires. Sew on hind legs, wire crossing 3/8" from back end of body wire. Place front legs so that the distance from wire to wire is 1¾". Arch hump pad and sew it to end of body and above front legs. Cut all loops. Bend into shape and trim with a pair of sharp scissors. Sew on ears and eyes, then embroider a mouth with a contrasting thread.

Panda. This little animal which comes from China is loved by everyone. Its body is white wool, the legs black and the eyes and ears are cut from black felt. Cut the body wire 9" long and the leg wires 7" long and bend in half. Make the body pad of white yarn and wind an extra layer or two as a Panda is a fat little animal. The legs, of course, are made with black wool. A Panda has black shoulders. This effect can be obtained by making a pad 2" long and ½" thick. After the body is finished, part the yarn across the shoulders from leg to leg and sew pad in place. Cut loops and trim to shape.

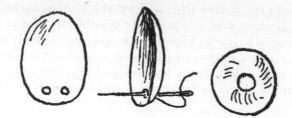

Figure 9. Detail of Panda Ear and Eye.

Cut two rounded ears from black felt in the shape illustrated in Figure 9. Form a cup shape by sewing around the edge or punching two holes at the bottom through which a thread is run. The eyes are made by sewing a black shoe button onto a round circle of black felt.

Figure 10. Donkey.

This little donkey is made in the same manner as the other animals, only it can be made from burlap ravelings as well as yarn. Since the donkey is almost a universal animal and loved by everyone, it is often made from natural materials such as thin grasses or raffia. The method of sewing and assembling the parts is the same.

To make a donkey—cut a body wire 16″ in length and two leg wires 12″. Bend them all in half. You will need to make the body and head along the same center wire but in different widths as you did the giraffe. See Figure 7. Make the body pad first and make it about 4″ long, saving the rest of the wire for neck and head. After the wire is sewed securely to body pad, remove rods, place them back in the jig nearer together and again make pads for the neck and head. When you make the leg pads, be sure to wrap all four ends with a dark grey yarn or string to suggest hoofs on the donkey.

Assemble the body and legs and sew together according to directions given in Figure 4. Sew the hind legs ⅜" from the end of the body wire. Place front legs on so that measuring from wire to wire the space between is 2½". When you sculpture to shape, be sure to leave some long strands at the top of the neck beginning in front of the ears for a mane.

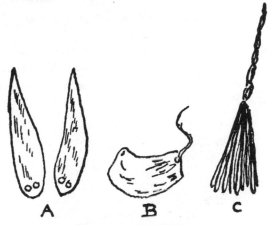

Figure 11. Donkey's Features.

A donkey's ears turn out from the head as shown in the above illustration. Be sure to set them down a little from the top and curve them as shown in Figure 11A. The hoof is shaped as shown in B, and C suggests a braided or twisted tail with a small tassel at the end.

If you want to make a donkey by using grass or raffia instead of wool, follow the same directions for sewing and shaping the body. The only thing you must know is that you wet the material and have it damp while the work is proceeding.

Index